ADVANCE PRAISE FOR SELLING BUILDINGS

"An absolute must-read for anyone serious about making money in commercial real estate. If you're an investor or broker, this powerful guide will empower you to achieve extraordinary success! Bob Knakal's record-breaking career and Rod Santomassimo's insights create the absolute roadmap for maximizing returns."
Barbara Corcoran, Founder of The Corcoran Group & Shark and Executive Producer on ABC's "Shark Tank"

"Bob Knakal and Rod Santomassimo have crafted a memoir and a how-to manual intertwined with stories, personalities, legends, successes, and heartbreak. For a real estate guy like me, it reads like an action thriller that rewards with practical how-to Advice. Bob is a friend of long-standing who is the undisputed heavyweight champion and who works his ass off on every deal. He's the best in the business. This sort of how-to tell all is a very generous gift to all who come after him."
Steven Roth / Vornado Realty Trust, Chairman and CEO

"Everyone's journey in real estate is unique, but the experiences and expertise that Bob shares in this book are a gift to anyone who aspires to have a long career in our industry and replicate even a small percentage of his success. He speaks candidly about his own strengths and weaknesses and offers a roadmap for how to navigate the inevitable challenges that arise in the world of commercial real estate."
Jeff Blau, CEO of Related Companies

"Packed with proven strategies from one of the all-time greats in real estate. Bob Knakal shares the secrets behind his record-breaking sales, and Rod Santomassimo adds actionable insights from decades of coaching. Together, they make this book an investment in your success."
Stephen Siegel, Chairman of Global Brokerage, CBRE

"This book offers invaluable insights for both seasoned professionals and newcomers alike to our industry from masters of their craft. Through their stories, Bob Knakal and Rod Santomassimo teach real lessons and make astute observations that anyone who wants to succeed in this business must know. Their innovative thinking, knowledge, and experience offer a roadmap for turning obstacles into opportunities."
Aby Rosen, Principal, RFR HOLDING LLC

Bob Knakal and Rod Santomassimo have written the real estate broker's bible. It should be required reading for anyone in the real estate business. The book's qualities are too many to list, but they include honesty, full transparency, sharing every sales and marketing strategy known to their profession, and forty years of entrepreneurial wisdom. Pure genius.
Francis Greenburger Times Equities

"In Selling Buildings, Bob Knakal and Rod Santomassimo exemplify the essence of the wingman philosophy—trust, mutual support, and an unwavering commitment to excellence. Their synergistic partnership offers readers a strategic flight plan to navigate the complexities of commercial real estate with confidence and precision. This book is a testament to how collaborative leadership and shared vision can elevate success in any mission."
Lt. Col. (Ret) Waldo Waldman, Hall of Fame Speaker and New York Times bestselling author of Never Fly Solo

"With over four decades of experience in New York City, Bob Knakal shares his hard-earned insights on maximizing value in the world's most competitive real estate market. As the commercial real estate industry undergoes a generational shift, Knakal's strategies for creating value, navigating uncertainty, and building long-term relationships are more essential than ever. This practical guide equips investors and brokers with a roadmap to success."
Scott Rechler, CEO and Chairman, RXR

"Bob Knakal's and Rod Santomassimo's takeaways from many fascinating New York deals are pure real estate gold. But it is the life lessons experienced along the way that give this book its soul. Fun to read, and lots to learn from this master of his craft."
Mary Ann Tighe, CEO, NY Tri-State Region CBRE

"In the vast ocean of commercial real estate information, it's extraordinary to have one of the greatest brokers of all time candidly share his insights. Bob has been in the middle of some of the biggest deals in New York City history, and his journey from humble beginnings to the top of the world's most competitive real estate market is a blueprint for success. In collaboration with Rod, his personal broker coach, they generously reveal the principles and practices that have earned them universal respect in real estate. Having access to such profound knowledge early in my career would have been a game-changer."
Don Tepman, President and Founder of TownCentre Capital, "StripMallGuy"

$ELLING BUILDING$

Maximizing Prices and Profits
in
Commercial Real Estate

BOB KNAKAL &
ROD SANTOMASSIMO

Selling Buildings

Domus Publishing
ISBN PB: 979-8-9929001-0-1
Also Available in eBook

Book Cover by Inco MediaPromotion
Book design by Variance Author Services
www.varianceauthorservices.com

$ELLING BUILDING$

Maximizing Prices and Profits
in
Commercial Real Estate

Bob Knakal &
Rod Santomassimo

ACKNOWLEDGMENTS

This book would not have been possible without the help of our writing coach, Wally Bock. Everyone needs a coach to achieve greater success, and Wally is simply the best.

Thank you, Wally.

FOREWORD
BY
RYAN SERHANT

In the dynamic world of real estate, especially here in New York, there are few names that resonate as profoundly as Bob Knakal's. With a career that spans four decades, Bob has brokered the sale of over 2,342 properties in New York City, amassing a market value of approximately $22 billion. By the time you read this, those numbers will be higher.

I'm proud to call Bob a friend, a client, and a mentor. His innovative approach, especially the territorial system he implemented at Massey Knakal Realty Services, revolutionized the industry and established new benchmarks for excellence.

Bob has raised industry standards and redefined excellence and professionalism. His deep understanding of market dynamics and an unwavering commitment to his clients have solidified his reputation as a paragon of success in the real estate arena. But beyond the numbers, what truly sets Bob apart is his ability to innovate and inspire. He has always been ahead of the curve, identifying trends and opportunities before others even recognized their existence. From understanding the nuances of zoning laws to predicting shifts in market demand, Bob's insights have helped shape the trajectory of New York City's real estate landscape.

Bob's contributions go beyond his own deals. He has dedicated much of his career to mentoring the next generation of brokers, sharing his knowledge and strategies to help others succeed. His influence can be seen in the countless professionals who credit their success to his guidance. Bob's approach to mentorship is rooted in his belief that real estate is more than just transactions—it's about building communities and fostering connections that endure.

Complementing Bob's practical prowess is the unparalleled expertise of Rod Santomassimo, arguably the most accomplished coach in the commercial real estate sector. As the founder and president of the Massimo Group, Rod has dedicated his career to empowering brokers and agents, equipping them with the tools and strategies necessary to excel in a competitive marketplace. His innovative coaching methodologies have transformed the careers of countless professionals, fostering a culture of continuous improvement and excellence.

This book represents the confluence of Bob's extensive real-world experience and Rod's strategic coaching acumen. It offers readers a unique opportunity to glean insights from two of the commercial real estate industry's most influential figures. Whether you're a seasoned investor who is considering selling your commercial building, a commercial real estate broker aiming to elevate your practice, or someone who simply wants to understand what makes a great deal, the lessons encapsulated within these pages serve as a comprehensive guide to navigating the complexities of commercial real estate.

Readers should view this book not just as a manual but as an invitation to learn from a master of the craft. Bob Knakal's approach to real estate is a masterclass in innovation, perseverance, and success. His methods have been tested and proven in one of the most competitive markets in the world. Rod Santomassimo's "Massimo Methods" have significantly impacted the lives and businesses of commercial real estate brokers across the globe. The lessons here are not theoretical; they are rooted in decades of practical experience and hard-earned wisdom.

I am honored to contribute this foreword, recognizing the invaluable contributions of both Bob and Rod to our industry. Their combined wisdom and dedication to advancing the profession make this book essential for anyone committed to achieving excellence in commercial real estate.

So, as you turn these pages, be prepared to gain insights that can transform your understanding of real estate. Whether you aspire to close your first deal or redefine your entire career, the knowledge contained in this book is a roadmap to excellence. Bob Knakal's legacy is one of impact, and through this book, he invites you to share that legacy.

Ryan Serhant
CEO and Founder, SERHANT.

SELLING BUILDINGS

HOW TO MAXIMIZE PRICES AND PROFITS IN COMMERCIAL REAL ESTATE

INTRODUCTION BY ROD SANTOMASSIMO

What does it take to not just sell commercial real estate for the maximum price but also create a legacy within the world of commercial real estate brokerage? This question has intrigued me since I started my coaching business, The Massimo Group, with our mission of helping brokers create successful businesses and a great quality of life. Over the years, I've discovered that the answer is a mix of expertise, discipline, innovation, and an unrelenting commitment to excellence. These traits define the best brokers, as will the principles that you'll find in the pages of this book.

And no one exemplifies these qualities better than Bob Knakal.

Bob Knakal isn't just a name in commercial real estate—he's a legend. Over his remarkable 40-year career, Bob has set records that few brokers could even dream of matching. He's sold over 2,300 buildings, likely more than any other individual broker in the history of New York City. He co-founded Massey Knakal Realty Services, a boutique brokerage that not only competed with, but outperformed national giants in one of the world's most competitive markets. By the time they sold the firm for $100 million to Cushman & Wakefield, it had become a household name among brokers and property owners alike.

But Bob's story is about more than numbers. It's about the transformation—of himself, his clients, and an entire industry. This book is your backstage pass to the deals, decisions, and defining moments of his career. It's also a playbook for anyone who wants to maximize value, whether you're a property owner looking to sell or a broker determined to dominate your market.

The Journey to Becoming the Best

Bob's path to the top started with a mix of curiosity, hard work, and frankly, a bit of luck. A Wharton School graduate with ambitions of becoming the next Wall Street titan, Bob discovered commercial real estate almost by accident. He quickly realized that his passion for numbers, coupled with his relentless drive, made brokerage the perfect fit.

But success didn't come easy. In his first years at Coldwell Banker, Bob faced rejection after rejection, cold-calling property owners who had no interest in selling or even talking to him. Yet he persevered, developing a meticulous approach to prospecting and client outreach. This discipline laid the foundation for his later success, and it's one of the first lessons you'll encounter in this book: the power of consistent, value-driven prospecting.

Early in his career, Bob partnered with Paul Massey, and together they built something extraordinary. They created a brokerage model rooted in geographic territory expertise, where brokers became specialists in specific neighborhoods. This approach wasn't just innovative—it was revolutionary. It allowed them to provide unparalleled value to clients and fostered a culture of collaboration that remains an undisputed blueprint for success.

Lessons from the Front Lines

This book is filled with stories from Bob's career that highlight the strategies, challenges, and insights that made him a leader in the field. Take for example, his first deal. Bob and Paul worked tirelessly to find the right buyer, ultimately turning a "shitty assignment" into their first commission. Then, there was a fire in the building the night before closing. What happened next? You'll find out in the pages that follow. The deal was a lesson in persistence and creativity—two traits that every successful broker needs to cultivate.

Or consider the story of Bob's breakthrough with Harry Macklowe, one of New York's most prominent developers. After two years of unanswered calls and ignored mailings, Bob finally got through to Harry—by sheer luck. That initial conversation led to a relationship that would produce multiple deals, including a $179 million portfolio sale. The lesson? Relationships are built over time, and persistence always pays off.

The stories in this book aren't just about deals—they're about people. Bob's work with clients like Harry Macklowe, Richard Parkoff, and others reveal the human side of brokerage. It's about understanding what motivates people, solving their problems, and earning their trust. Whether it's helping a property owner navigate a family dispute or guiding a developer through a complex zoning issue, Bob's ability to connect with clients on a personal level is a hallmark of his success.

Building a Legacy

One of the most inspiring aspects of Bob's career is how he used his success to elevate others. At Massey Knakal, he and Paul created a culture that emphasized training, mentorship, and self-improvement. Every new hire went through an intensive onboarding program designed to make them market experts. Weekly training sessions ensured that even the most seasoned brokers continued to grow. This focus on education wasn't just good for the team—it was good for the business.

Bob's philosophy was simple: *If you invest in people, they'll invest in you.* This principle is reflected in the long list of Massey Knakal alumni who have gone on to leadership positions or started their own firms. It's also evident in Bob's commitment to philanthropy and community involvement, which have earned him as much respect as his brokerage achievements.

Thriving in the Ups and Downs

Commercial real estate is a cyclical business, and Bob's career has been shaped by its highs and lows. From the Savings and Loan Crisis of the 1980s to the Great Recession of 2008 to the Pandemic, Bob has navigated some of the most challenging markets in history. What sets him apart is his ability to adapt.

During downturns, Bob and Paul doubled down on their strategies, hiring top talent and expanding into new territories when others were pulling back. It was a bold move, but it paid off. When the market rebounded, Massey Knakal was perfectly positioned to capitalize on the recovery. The lesson here is clear: success comes to those who prepare, even when the odds seem stacked against them.

As of the writing of this book:

- Bob Knakal has sold more buildings, 2,342, than any broker in New York City's history. And one could project more than any single broker on the planet. Now, understand that most of these sales were when he worked for his boutique firm and beat out the much larger and established national firms, making his track record even more impressive.

- He has won more awards, including both real estate-related awards and humanitarian awards, than any broker I am aware of. Bob and his former partner, Paul Massey, built and bootstrapped an independent boutique commercial real estate firm that dominated the New York City brokerage landscape for over 26 years. The company regularly sold more buildings than their national competition by 3X! They sold the company for $100 million.
- Bob developed a Territory System that was not only a better approach for their commercial agents but also better for their clients. This system changed the way brokerages look at the market today.
- Bob has mentored hundreds of commercial agents. As of the writing of this book, 31 of his former colleagues have gone on to own or lead brokerage divisions in New York City.
- He developed The Knakal Map Room and his "AlmaKnakal" reports, the most comprehensive market research platform in New York City. The Knakal Map Room attracts investors and developers from all over the world.
- Bob recently founded BRKEA Advisors. This advisory/brokerage firm combines four decades of brokerage experience, market information, and today's leading artificial intelligence to assist their clients in making the most prudent investment

decisions and maximizing their property's sales value.

The Structure of This Book

This book is designed to give you actionable insights you can apply immediately. Each chapter focuses on a specific aspect of brokerage or property sales, illustrated by real-world examples from Bob's career. From mastering the art of negotiation to understanding market trends, you'll gain a comprehensive understanding of what it takes to succeed.

Within several of the chapters Bob will outline a Client Success Story. These stories will help you contextually understand the time, environment and challenges of the market and the parties involved. After each Client Success Story, "Bob will share his "BK's Takeaways for Investors", and I will share my *"Rod's Lessons for Brokers."* Please read each, regardless of your position in this equation.

In sections that I felt needed some additional context, you will see "Rod's Reflections," and at the end of each chapter, you'll find "Rod's Wrap-Up," where I distill the key lessons into practical takeaways. These insights are drawn from Bob's experiences and also from my work coaching thousands of brokers across North America.

Bob's sections will be displayed in plain text, *and my sections will be italicized.* That way, you will be clear about who is talking.

Together, we'll explore how to apply these principles to your own business, whether you're looking to close more deals, build a stronger team, or maximize the value of your commercial property.

A Call to Action

This book isn't just a collection of stories and advice—it's a call to action. Whether you're a broker striving to dominate your market or a property owner seeking to maximize your return, the lessons in these pages are a roadmap to achieving your goals. But remember, success isn't about luck or shortcuts. It's about discipline, persistence, and a willingness to learn.

Bob Knakal's career is proof that greatness is possible when you combine talent with hard work and a relentless focus on adding value. As you read this book, I challenge you to think about how you can apply these lessons to your journey. What would it take for you to become the Bob Knakal of your market?

Turn the page, and let's find out.

LEARNING THE BUSINESS

Bob didn't want to be a commercial real estate broker, at least not while in high school or during his first year at the Wharton School at the University of Pennsylvania, where he focused mainly on pitching for its varsity baseball team and learning as much as he could to become the next Ivy League Wall Street success.

But that changed and changed quickly. He accidentally discovered commercial real estate and realized his knack for numbers and natural traits were a great fit for the industry.

In this chapter, you'll go back to the beginning of a career that changed the landscape of investment sales in New York City forever. You'll learn about what Bob did to achieve astonishing success in his first years in the business. And you'll discover the "secret" of success in commercial real estate.

~

How I Got Into Commercial Real Estate by Accident

July 16, 1984, was my first day on the job. I graduated from Wharton and was living in the house I grew up in, in Maywood, New Jersey, with just my dad as my mom had passed away at the end of my junior year. The night before that first day, I shined my shoes and picked out the suit I would wear. That wasn't much of a challenge. I only owned two suits and five permanent press shirts.

At 5:30 am, I caught the first bus to the city. During the ride, I thought about how I got there. When I first got to Wharton, I wanted to be an investment banker in New York City like everybody else in my class. The summer after my first year, I was looking for an internship that would look good on my resume to help me achieve my goal.

I had just dropped my resume off at a Paine Webber office, and across the hall, I saw what I thought was another bank. I walked into a Coldwell Banker office, asked if they were hiring for the summer, and dropped my resume off. When they called later that day to set up an interview for the following day, I immediately set it up. I didn't find out it was a real estate company until the following morning at the library, where I went to get information on this "bank" I had never heard of. No one else was hiring, so I reluctantly took the job. I immediately loved the business – everything about it. Looking at buildings, talking to people on the phone, meeting interesting people. The brokers were all really happy, and I was excited. But I was still not completely sold. That would change.

During my sophomore year, a Wharton grad was a guest speaker in my entrepreneurial management class. He said, "I was sitting right where you are 20 years ago. I wanted to be an investment banker, and I know most of you want that, too. Do something you love and have passion for." He told us how much he loved selling pet food and that his passion for it led to success, and that success led to a lot of money. "I'm the happiest guy I know because I chose to do what I really love, not because I thought I would make a lot of money doing it. If you are successful, the money will follow."

This advice hit me hard. I decided right then that I wanted to go into commercial real estate. Subsequently, I took every real estate course Penn offered. I gave up my dreams of becoming a legendary investment banker. Instead, I would become a legendary commercial real estate broker. I worked at Coldwell Banker during the following two summers. Toward the end of the third summer, the head of the Jersey office offered me a full-time position after graduation. I thanked them for the offer but had the guts/nerve to ask if they could introduce me to the CB folks in New York City so I could also interview there. They did, and I did. The guys in New York City offered me a position and I took the job in the Big Apple.

As a kid, our family would go into Manhattan to visit my grandparents every month or two. My eyes bulged out of my head, looking at all those big buildings. Wow! I wanted to be there. Before I knew it, I was headed in for my first day.

My First Day

My bus pulled into Port Authority around 6:00 a.m. I took the subway to 53rd and Madison and then walked down to 49th. I took the elevator up to the fourth floor. It was 6:20.

The hallway was dark, and the office doors were locked. OK, what do I do now? I sat on the floor and waited. About five minutes later, this guy, who looked to be around my age, showed up and unlocked the door. That guy was Paul Massey. I met Paul at a CB event the previous summer. Although we only chatted for a short time, I remembered meeting him. He was startled by me sitting there in the dark. We said hello and walked into the office. I sure didn't have any vision of what was ahead for us.

I sat in the reception area for about a half hour, waiting for the managing broker to show up. He basically said, "Hey, welcome aboard. Here's your desk." In the office, about fifty brokers focused on office leasing, 15 on retail leasing, and only four pursued investment sales. I knew I wanted to be in the building sales department. Besides Paul, the three other investment sales guys all had about 20 years of experience. And they wanted nothing to do with Paul or me.

The boss says, "Paul Massey just got out of the training program. Follow him around. He'll show you where the supply closet and coffee machine are. If you have any questions, ask him, but go sell buildings." That was my training program. Go sell buildings.

The Start of a Beautiful Partnership

So, I hung out with Paul, and we talked about how we were going to do things, and literally, on day two, we were having lunch, and we're like, "Hey, these other guys aren't really paying a lot of attention to us. Why don't we just work together? Let's partner up and split everything 50/50 and see how it goes?"

Paul and I were the two youngest kids in the office, but we quickly figured out what it took to be successful. We were the first ones in the office almost every day, and we were there relatively late. I left the office around 6:30 every night to get home, go directly to the gym, and prepare for the next day. I was eating dinner around 10 o'clock at night. It really wasn't a healthy thing. My routine was simple. I'd work, workout, eat dinner, go right to sleep, and get up in time to catch that 5:30 bus.

The First Exclusive

I remember the first exclusive we ever got was on 115 East 55th Street, a little four-story commercial office townhouse owned by a guy named John Coleman. His main business was owning hotels. He owned several Ritz Carlton hotels and ran his business out of the building. He was one of the first cold calls we made because he was in our territory—more on that later.

To our surprise, he agreed to meet with Paul and me. We met with him, saw the building, and put together a Broker Opinion of Value (BOV). He was reluctant to hire us. We were two young kids, barely shaving and had never sold a building. We reviewed three years of neighborhood comp sales with him and demonstrated that we knew the market. We reviewed everything else on the market that his building would compete with. We kept telling him he would be our top priority (he would be our *only* priority), and this deal would mean more to us than to any other broker. He was interested but reluctant.

Coleman was always well-dressed, really, very sharp. So, Paul and I got our shoes shined every time before we went to meet with this guy to make a good impression. We probably met with him seven or eight times to talk about it. Finally, he cracked. He hired us maybe because he thought, "Geez, if these guys are going after me so hard, maybe they'll go after the buyers so hard."

I remember how great it felt to get that exclusive listing signed. Then, we put a For Sale sign on the building, which was a novel approach in New York then. Signs on properties were generally used by residential brokers. People were like, "What the heck are you doing putting that sign up there?" Hey, we want everybody to know the buildings are for sale. We then sent out a mailing to all the other brokers in New York City, and they were like, "You'll cooperate with us. Wow." Nobody proactively did that before." No one was doing that then, but it made sense to us, and more importantly, it was in our client's best interest, so we did it. And it changed how building sales were being done in NY in the middle market space.

CLIENT SUCCESS STORY: FIRE SALE: THE UNEXPECTED FIRST DEAL

Our first closing was in April of '85. Here's the story. Two fellows from Atlanta came into our Coldwell Banker office and said, "Hey, we've worked with CB around the country. We need a building in New York." American Medical International (AMI) wanted a building to house the first MRI facility in New York. The challenge was their building couldn't be near a subway because the magnetic field would get screwed up by the subways going by. I think our boss thought, "Oh, this is a low-probability, shitty assignment. Let's give it to the two young kids."

As it turns out, this was one of only two "buyer rep" deals I would do in my career. Paul and I would later create fundamental guidelines for working with property owners that would be in our best interest and theirs as well.

The physical requirements for the ideal property were such that there were not a lot of options. We called every broker in town looking for deals and scoured the NY Times classified section, which was the multiple listings platform of its day. We only came up with five or six buildings that met the requirements. We toured all the properties with the buyers and made offers on two of them. One wasn't accepted, and the offer was so low that the seller wouldn't even make a counteroffer. The other offer was for 1421 Third Avenue.

After two months of negotiating, the property owner accepted AMI's offer and signed the contract. We thought we were guaranteed a fee. But literally the day before the closing, we got a call from the seller's broker, and he said, "Hey guys, I've got some really bad news. We had a fire in the building last night, and the first two floors of the building are charred." And we're like, "Oh no, you've got to be kidding! We were so excited. This is our first sale". We sucked it up and called the buyer. To our shock and surprise, he wasn't upset! "No big deal. It'll save me money on the demolition costs," he said.

We were at the closing the next day, and the closing room was relatively small. So, you've got attorneys in there, you've got the AMI guys, you've got the seller, and the title closer, and there's no room for us. So, we sat in the reception area, which was just outside the closing room.

The door to the room is open. We are there at 10 o'clock in the morning, and the hours go by. When they serve lunch, they have us come in to grab a sandwich. We returned to the reception area, sat, ate, and waited. No cell phones to use or emails to look at back in those days. We just sat and waited. We waited for hours, and I was nervously flipping this penny I found in my pocket the entire time. Between the waiting and my coin tossing, Paul breaks and shouts at me to stop playing with my damn penny!

Then, we hear this screaming. This seller was a very hotheaded woman who wasn't going to be told what to do. Very difficult, yelling, yelling, yelling. About three o'clock, she comes running out of the room screaming, "I'm not closing, I'm not closing. You can't have my building. You can't have my building". Her attorneys are coming, grabbing her, saying, "No, come on. Come on." They're trying to calm her down and pulling her back into the room.

Paul and I are sitting there like deer in the headlights looking at this. What the heck is going on? Is this what the real estate business is really like? The building almost burns down, and our client still wants to close! What's the issue? Finally, the attorneys calm her down. She goes back into the room. The problem was something about some kind of adjustment that the buyer was looking for some relief on. It was like a minor thing, like a sidewalk violation or something like that. And finally, the buyer agreed to pay for the violation. They went in and closed the deal. They come out, and the closing attorney says, "Hey guys, we closed. Here's your check."

I remember our feet didn't touch the ground as we walked up Madison Avenue back to the office; we were so excited. Sitting at our desks, in the glow of the deal, I reached into my pocket. And hey, in my pocket is the penny I'd been flipping. I thought to myself, "This is a lucky penny." I taped it to my desk, and that lucky penny has been taped to every desk I have worked from ever since.

We decided to do a tombstone ad and send it out to everybody who owned buildings in our territory. This was a printed announcement about the sale. Remember, we didn't have social media or property blasts back then. We mailed it out, as we would for every one of our sales from then on. The commission Paul and I made on that deal was $12,500 each. Surely, we must be the richest guys in New York City we thought to ourselves! I immediately went out and bought a couple more suits and a bunch of shirts.

The big insight from that first sale was how lucky we were. And that you can't make a career out of luck.

Here are three key takeaways from this deal story for commercial real estate investors and brokers.

BK's Takeaways for Investors:

Look Past Surface Issues

AMI showed flexibility when the building had fire damage. They saw an opportunity in the damage ("save money on demolition costs"). Focus on fundamental property attributes (location away from subways for MRI equipment) and don't let minor issues (sidewalk violations) derail the deal

Work with Market Experts

AMI succeeded by leveraging Coldwell Banker's network. They found a property that met very specific requirements (away from subway lines). They benefited from brokers who thoroughly canvassed the market. They received access to all available options through broker cooperation.

Be Solution-Oriented in Negotiations

When issues arose at closing, the resolution came through compromise. The buyer agreed to pay for a violation to close the deal. They maintained focus on the big picture rather than minor details. They demonstrated flexibility to achieve the desired outcome.

Rod's Lessons for Brokers:

Territory Specialization Matters

Focus on becoming an expert in a specific area. This doesn't have to be a geographic area. Know every building, owner, and transaction in your area of specialization. Use this expertise to differentiate yourself, even if you are a newcomer. Deep market knowledge helps overcome a lack of experience.

Consistent Prospecting is Key

Bob and Paul made consistent cold calls and mailings. As you'll learn later in this book, that presence-building and prospecting continued in good times and bad. They used innovative marketing (signs, tombstone ads, mailings). They were persistent and met with the first client 7-8 times before they secured the exclusive listing.

Professional Presentation is Critical
Bob and Paul dressed professionally despite limited resources (Bob only had two suits). They shined their shoes before every client meeting. They also prepared detailed market analyses for presentations. They demonstrated thoroughness in knowing comps and competing properties

These takeaways reflect how both sides of the transaction can benefit from professional representation, market knowledge, and a focus on solutions rather than problems.

Rod's Analysis

Bob was lucky with that first closing. He was lucky that their broker gave them this opportunity, although everyone knew it was a "shitty" assignment. He was lucky their client didn't freak out, let alone back out when the building caught fire a day before the closing. And he was lucky the closing team could calm down the seller and get her to close. But luck is no way to sell buildings. Luck is not a strategy. Bob and Paul knew this. They would have to make a career out of higher probability work.

~

Knowing Your Territory Gives You an Edge

I knew we were onto something good. Focusing on a specific geographic territory gave us an advantage over our competitors. This market expertise positioned us as market authorities despite our inexperience. We were able to secure exclusive listings, and over the next year, we would sell five more buildings, six in all, over the first eighteen months in the business. We were getting exclusives and closing deals. CB was having other brokers come in from other offices around the country to talk to us to find out what we were doing that got such good results. That didn't mean everything was going well, though.

CB's policy was that if a deal was in your territory, you got a piece of it. During that second year, the guys with all the experience went to our managing broker and said, "Hey, we have this deal. It's in Bob and Paul's territory. We don't want to bring them in." The boss weaseled out and didn't make them bring us in, which pissed us off. I'll share more about that shortly.

The Secret to Commercial Real Estate Success

One thing our managing broker couldn't do was ignore our success. Within two years, Paul and I were officially named the directors of the Investment Sales Group in New York City. That meant those guys with all that experience were working for us. Yep, it felt a little like a Wolf of Wall Street moment. We were the young guns outperforming the old guys. Except, unlike Jordan Belfort, Paul and I would build our success on ethics, integrity, market knowledge and first and foremost, a client-first mentality. The future looked bright for us, even though there would be twists and turns in the road that we couldn't anticipate.

People always ask me, "What's the secret to succeeding in commercial real estate?" Most of them are looking for magic, some way to succeed without working too hard. There is no magic. This is a simple business. It's simple, but hard. It's not a complicated business. We're not using the theory of relativity. We're not curing cancer. We are just selling buildings for people.

It is a business that requires expertise - to differentiate yourself from everyone else, passion - to push you through the tough times and keep you on track, and most importantly, discipline – to continue doing some very mundane things over and over. It's like one step above somebody who's on a conveyor belt like Lucille Ball with the chocolates. You can Google it if you don't know what I am talking about. It's very monotonous, fundamental, and basic stuff. But you must have the discipline to do it over and over and over to demonstrate market presence. Abraham Lincoln once said, "Discipline is choosing between what you want now and what you want most." Those who succeed the most in commercial real estate use discipline brilliantly to focus on what they want most.

~

Rod's Wrap-up

Bob's entry into commercial real estate may have been a mistake, but his initial success was no accident. Bob talks about discipline, and he exemplified this early. He got up at 4:45, got to the bus by 5:30, and the office by 6:30. He then worked at least 12 hours before commuting back home, working out, and getting some dinner before going to bed. Bob would tell you he still "only works half a day. It just depends on which 12 hours it is."

Bob's acceptance and, in fact, insistence on a territorial-based system, where brokers are responsible for understanding every owner, building, and transaction in a specific market area would become a pillar of his and his firm's market dominance.

In commercial real estate brokerage, it is commonly thought that how quickly you have your first actual closing is not as important as how quickly you can have a second closing. While Bob's second closing occurred over six months from his first, he and Paul would close five more deals in the following six months. This flurry of deals was predicated on Bob and Paul's persistence in prospecting calls and mailings and, of course, ensuring they were the CRE authority in their market.

Bob is not afraid to try new things. One of my favorite sayings is, "You either define the change, or you are defined by the change." Bob and Paul defined changes early on by using signs to promote buildings, tombstones to promote sales, and cooperating with competitors to ensure their clients received the highest and most qualified offers for their buildings.

As you will see throughout this book, Bob will continue to define change throughout his career. Changes were not only good for his business but also for his property owner clients.

A BUSINESS IS BORN

As much as you want things to work out, sometimes they just don't. While Bob and Paul were now "in charge," they were still asking for permission and approval to grow the business they wanted to grow.

As Bob will tell you, there comes a time when enough is enough, and the best thing you can do is proactively prepare for that time.

We really liked it at CB and wanted to stay there. The folks we worked with in the trenches, the producers we were in the cubes with, were fantastic people. CB was the new kid on the block in New York City, and the underdog role bound us together. The "us against the world" perspective was motivating and would also motivate us at Massey Knakal.

Success at CB

Our efforts at CB were bearing fruit, and being named heads of the group felt great, but the prior lack of support from management to uphold the integrity of the system was still a pebble in our shoes.

Paul and I were now in charge of Investment Sales for New York, and things were going great. The old guys weren't a problem. Two of them left soon after we were put in charge. As soon as we were named leaders of the investment division, we brought in a whole bunch of new young guys that were kicking ass, and we were having fun.

Our passion for the business and the hours we were putting in translated into great things. In our second year, Paul and I each made $176,000. We felt like we were the richest guys in the world. And like most brokers who start making money and were concerned about senior management's decisions, we thought to ourselves, “We should start our own firm.” The problem was we didn’t have the capital to start a business. But that wouldn’t deter us. All we had to do was get a loan. We thought, “Hey, we make $176,000, they'll give us whatever we want.” So, off we went to the bank to get a loan to start our business.

All We Have To Do Is Get a Loan

Our banker was a woman named Nancy Stockwell, the branch manager at Chemical Bank at 47th Street and Madison Avenue. We had a great relationship with her, and she could not have been nicer to us. She had been at the bank for decades and still wore one of those 1970s hairdos that was very high and plastered down with an entire can of Aqua Net hair spray. My mom had the same.

We walked into the bank, confident that we just had to ask for the loan, would be given an application, sign it, and get the loan. Were we mistaken! We calculated that we needed about $500,000 to start the business, so that’s what we asked for.

To our dismay, Nancy sympathetically, but with a big smile on her face, explained that we would have to go out, start the business, and come back with a three-year track record to discuss some type of revolving credit line. Ouch! What a letdown. We had no collateral and no family members who could provide any funding or credit enhancement, so we walked back to the office completely deflated. We were just 24 and 26 years old and needed to face our reality. This was the first adversity we faced and would be good practice for dealing with the adversities to come.

Maybe We Should Stay at CB

With our hats in our hands, we said, "You know what? Maybe rather than going and starting our own company, let's see if CB will make a separate profit center for our investment sales division and give us a piece of it." After all, we were running the division, hiring folks, training the producers. It would be a natural fit. So, we put together a business plan – complete with a strategic plan, spreadsheets, projections, etc. My Wharton School training was useful here.

We laid out the whole thing. This plan would eventually become the Massey Knakal blueprint. There was the territory system, guys working here, there, and everywhere. We didn't take the outer boroughs into consideration at the time, just Manhattan. We wanted to build teams; transactional associates. The whole concept was there.

We took the plan to our boss, Kurt Martin. We said, "Look, we're running these guys." We had the division up to 13 or 14 people at that time. We want to make investment sales its own profit center, and we'd like a piece of it. We asked for 10 percent of the profits of that business.

Kurt thought it was a good idea and would run it up the flagpole. He went to Jim Didion, the CEO of CB, who Kurt reported to directly, given the company's focus on the New York City market. Kurt came back to us and said that it was a no-go. It was understandable to us. If they made this deal with two young guys in New York, what would they have to do with other producers around the country who had more experience and much longer track records? A few months later, Kurt left CB to get on the principal side of the business and start buying properties.

In came a new boss, Matt Ochalski, from Chicago to run the New York operation. We met with Matt on his second day and began what would turn out to be a great relationship with him. Matt got it. He had heard about us and was very supportive. He was aware of our proposal and reiterated that it was a no-go.

How We Came Up with $400,000 to Start Massey Knakal

It was clear that our own profit center was not going to happen. That's when Paul and I knew we would have to come up with the money to start our own shop. So, we got to work on it.

CB was subletting the fourth floor at 437 Madison Avenue from DDB, which was a big advertising agency, and they had a subsidized cafeteria on the second floor. Part of our sublease deal was that CB employees could use the cafeteria, and it was like $1.50 for breakfast. Paul and I went down there and ate breakfast together every morning. I remember Paul had a gold Cross pen, and at least once a week he whipped that pen out and we wrote down all our deals that were under contract, how much we were going to make on each and how much money we could put aside from each one to fund the new company. It took us about two years to save up the money, putting some aside from every deal from the end of 1986, all of 1987, and most of 1988 to self-fund the start of our new business.

We thought we needed $500,000. Believe it or not, we ended up saving about $400,000 by the middle of 1988. Every time a commission check came in, we didn't pay ourselves, we paid our future selves. Sure, it was hard, making money and still living below your means for those years, and as it would turn out, many more years in the future. But if we wanted to start our own firm, there was no other way to get there, and we were ferociously focused on getting there.

Leaving CB

On November 15, 1988, we arranged a meeting with Matt to let him know we were going to leave. We wanted to do it the week before, but Matt was on vacation. The Monday after returning, he was swamped, so we arranged to have breakfast the following day at Prime Burger, a burger joint on East 51st Street around the corner from the office where Paul and I had lunch at least 3 days a week. They had awesome burgers, which we usually had with their tomato soup and a piece of spectacular pie. "Willie" had been there for decades and made homemade pies every day, which we loved. Sweet potato was my favorite!

Prime Burger also served breakfast, and we wanted to meet with Matt as soon as possible. With sweaty palms and lumps in our throats, we had to let our "friend" know that we would be leaving CB. Matt was clearly disappointed. After asking if there was anything he could do to change our minds, he asked what the firm's name would be. "Massey Knakal Realty Services," we said. The order of the names was determined via coin flips in the lobby of the Waldorf Astoria Hotel after a few drinks at Sir Harry's bar, named after Harry Helmsley, who once owned the storied hotel. It was the best four out of seven (just like the World Series). After I won the first flip, Paul won the next four in a row and the name was set. Thank goodness, because Knakal is so hard to spell, Knakal Massey would not have been optimal.

While disappointed, Matt made the transition relatively easy for us. What I didn't know until just a few months ago was that Matt, sensing that we were disenchanted, went to Didion to propose that Paul and I create and run "a real estate investment banking business" at CB, complete with our own and separate office space to take advantage of all the traction we were getting. Matt was shot down just as our prior boss, Kurt, had been. After we told Matt we were leaving, he called Didion to let him know, and his response was, "They'll be back here in six months."

Our Lean Startup

I've seen many brokers go out on their own and try to start big. Not us. Our first office was an 850-square-foot, 14-month sublease at 16 East 52nd Street, the listing for which we found in the NY Times classified section—the multiple listing system of its day. There were three of us: Paul, me, and a secretary, Tammy Clayton, who was ironically, Matt's secretary, with whom we had a great rapport.

We didn't even buy much office furniture. At the time, we were selling a mixed-use townhouse at 307 East 56th Street, with commercial spaces on the first two floors and residential apartments on the upper three floors. The building was owned by Eliba Levine, a writer of racy romance novels who inherited it from her father and dressed the part, often leaving little to the imagination.

The second-floor tenant was a travel agency that skipped out on their lease in the middle of the night, leaving an entire floor of travel brochures and old, beat-up furniture. We told Eliba that clearing out the space would make the building more marketable. We made a deal with her that we would clean it out ourselves if we could have the furniture. She agreed.

A couple of our friends from CB, Paul Edison and Kevin Danehy, along with Paul's brother-in-law, agreed to help us on a Saturday. It was a decision they likely regretted. We rented a U-Haul and thought it would take a couple of hours to make the move. Were we ever wrong! The building was a walk-up, so no elevator. Travel brochures are generally printed on heavy glossy stock and weigh a ton. I developed a new appreciation for movers and came to find out exactly how much heavy five-drawer lateral filing cabinets weigh. The move was a disaster, but about nine hours later, we had our start-up furniture in our new space.

Our First Exclusive Listings

So, now we are on our own, and Massey Knakal was born. On day two, we got the first two exclusive listings from a client named Dan Hirsch. We knew Dan, and during the first couple of days, we were sitting in the office dialing for dollars, telling people, "Hey, we just started our own firm, and we'd love to help you out with anything you need help with and blah, blah, blah."

I remember Dan saying, "It's perfect timing. I want to sell a couple of buildings." And we said, "Oh, great. Would you consider hiring us?" He knew we were just starting and said, "I love you guys. I don't care what company you're at. I'm hiring you, not the company." I will never forget that. And I was like, "Yeah, this is great."

Establishing a Market Presence

Getting the nod from Dan was a great feeling, but we knew we had to establish a market presence. That's what keeps you "top of mind" when a decision-maker decides it is time to transact. This was back in 1988 when social media didn't exist, and all we had was phone, hard mail, and print media.

We needed to keep clients and potential clients up to date on market trends and what we were up to with our fledgling firm. We created a Massey Knakal newsletter, which would typically consist of listings we were marketing, sales we just closed, and other market information that we thought owners would be interested in. It was all about delivering information of value to the client, and the newsletters did just that! We would go on to print it every quarter for over 26 years without missing a single quarter. Think about that—one hundred and six quarterly newsletters in a row. Many of these newsletters were saved and can be found in the "Writings" section on the BobKnakal.com website.

In addition, we sent monthly mailers to our client base. I estimate I stuffed over one million pieces of mail in my day—and I still have the paper cuts to prove it!

When it came to print media, how were two young kids with limited track records going to get coverage? Getting others to talk about you and hold you as an expert is much more impactful than talking about yourself. If you're getting a lot of press coverage, you look like an important player in the market. So, we attacked that issue strategically.

First, we made up a list of all the publications in New York City that covered commercial real estate. Then, we made up a list of all the reporters at those publications. We systematically called them, set up calls and meetings with them, pitched story ideas, and sent them mail about our activities. The thing to remember about members of the press is that they are constantly looking for story ideas. Proactively feeding them ideas is likely to get you quoted in their articles.

Back in those days, The Real Estate Weekly (REW) was the top real estate publication in the market. We called Roxanne Donovan, the editor of REW, and asked her to have lunch with us - at Prime Burger (where else). We had lunch, talked about what we were doing, nurtured the relationship, and many months later, Roxanne wrote a profile on us in the REW. We were on top of the world, made thousands of copies of that article, and sent it to everyone we had an address for. A copy of this profile can also be found on the BobKnakal.com website.

After decades of this process of engaging with the media, cultivating relationships, and feeding story ideas, our relationships were deep. When reporters moved on from one publication, they generally went to another one, so the relationships continued. These relationships resulted in me getting quoted in the media regularly - over 2,000 times per year -became commonplace! This old-school method of establishing market presence worked back then and still works today. However, today we have so many more ways to establish market presence than we did back then.

Those first couple of years were exciting. Right off the bat, Paul and I knew our partnership would work, and in the beginning, we did everything together. We ate breakfast and lunch together every day. Dinner probably twice a week. We were literally inseparable. There were very few "days off" and never "eight-hour days." We were building a business. We had a passion for it and believed in our approach, and our partnership was the strong bond we needed to build a strong foundation for Massey Knakal.

Rod's Wrap-Up

There is nothing more exciting than starting your own business. It's a lot like when you invest in your first property. You have all the dreams of independence and massive financial success, but most times, that dream quickly evaporates into long hours, more than imagined failures and intense struggles.

Fortunately, Bob and Paul did not let the challenges deter them from realizing their vision or initial success. Consider some of the essential business-building elements they pursued in the early days of Massey Knakal.

Sacrifice—Could you set a vision for 3 to 4 years out and have the discipline to do what is necessary to put off what you want today for what you truly want for tomorrow? *Continuing to live with his father for the first couple of years, commuting to New York City, and working long hours, all while he had money in the bank to change his current situation. He could live in the City, buy more suits, and generally have a better life. Instead, he sacrificed his present and made an extreme commitment to his future.*

You are your brand – this is a big one. *As Bob learned in the first week of Massey Knakal and would relearn throughout his career with Massey Knakal, Cushman & Wakefield, JLL, and now, BKREA – the client picks the broker more than they pick the firm. This is particularly true when you are dealing with families and high-net-worth individuals, as Bob often was. Yes, the organization you align with is important, and it must have a solid reputation, but ultimately, you are your brand.*

Playing the press – I wonder if you know every local, regional, and potentially national reporter and publication that can help you become a market authority. *Bob realized it's not who you know, but who knows you, early in his career. Bob is truly the "Prince of Presence" in New York City real estate. It's not by accident. Bob and Paul had a solid strategic plan and executed it religiously.*

Marketing Consistency – Massey Knakal became a marketing machine, constantly and consistently putting out physical

content way before digital and social outlets existed. *Still today, Bob relies on regular physical mailings to 1,000 building owners and market influencers. Yes, he has expanded into digital channels, but regardless of the channel, we have a delivery cadence. We know what happens daily, weekly, monthly, and quarterly.*

ALL BEGINNINGS ARE HARD

When the head of CB said, "They'll be back here in six months," he was playing the odds. The number one reason they fail is because they run out of cash. In commercial real estate brokerage, the sales cycle is long, and thus, if you don't have much cash, you better have lots of credit.

While starting a business is hard enough, starting just before the onset of a major economic downturn exponentially decreases the likelihood of success. And the Savings and Loan Crisis was just around the corner.

In this chapter, you'll learn how Bob and Paul endured hard times, laying the foundation for Massey Knakal to become a force in New York City real estate.

You'll learn how Bob and Paul built a solid business with diligent and disciplined attention to the basics. You'll also learn how they were innovative and resilient. You'll hear about a creative deal that helped keep MK going and about hairspray's role in keeping the firm afloat.

But let's start this chapter with the foundation for everything else. Bob and Paul had a remarkable partnership. They formed it on the second day after they met, and it lasted for 30 years. It was the core of a firm that blazed new trails and withstood many challenges. I asked Bob about what made the partnership special.

~

Effective Partnerships

I haven't studied partnerships. I've seen a lot of them come and go. Mostly, they're very short-term. I think one of the main reasons our partnership worked so well was because our work ethic was identical. The other was that we thought about the business in precisely the same way.

Those were the days when you couldn't work from home. There were no cell phones or high-speed internet access to allow productive work to be done while commuting or in your living room. When you left the office in those days, you were out of business. So, we would work in the office, twelve hours a day and most Saturdays and Sundays. I bet if you added up all the hours that Paul worked and all the hours I worked over the course of our 30-year partnership, there would be less than a 10-hour difference in the total number of hours. And I think that was a fundamental key to what made the partnership work. We had the same discipline and work ethic.

The other key aspect of our partnership was that we were completely aligned with respect to how we viewed the business of investment sales brokerage and interacting with clients. From the importance of prospecting to knowing we were in the information business and the integrity of that information was paramount to putting the client's interest ahead of our own, our perspective was unified. We were both fair and reasonable. We thought the same way. You know, there's a difference between thinking similar things and thinking the same way.

There are dozens of examples where one of our salespeople would come to me and say, "Hey, Bob, I have this circumstance. The seller said this. The buyer said this. I don't know what to do. How do I handle this?" And then they'd go to Paul and ask him, and he'd give the same exact answer that I did.

So, I think there was a commonality in how we approached the business, thought about the business, and our philosophy about the business, which is that it's a marathon, not a sprint. Don't worry about today's deal. Worry about what's right for the client. It'll always come back to you. I think that was an underlying thing. I totally, totally trusted him and believed that his interest was the same as mine.

The Savings and Loan Crisis

The stock market crashed in October of 1987; bank failures peaked in 1988, and by the end of the Savings & Loan Crisis, over 1,000 banks had failed. Banks with defaulted mortgages began a lengthy foreclosure process. Despite all this, the real estate market in New York City was still pretty good in 1988. Our investment sales market didn't crash until early 1989, and then the volume of sales really started to dry up. Oh boy!!

The RTC, the Resolution Trust Corporation, was formed to take over the properties that all these failed banks had taken back or were in the process of taking back, and those properties didn't really come to the market in any significant way until they started to dribble into the market in 1991.

Hard Times

That was a tough time. Overall, it was worse than the Great Financial Crisis in 2008 and 2009. But back in 1988, in the moment, as we were planning to leave CB, negotiating our lease and all that kind of stuff, it wasn't so bad. Then, the volume of sales slowed down in 1989, and nothing was moving. We would make our eight property owner connections for the day (our goal then) and got nothing positive out of those calls. It was really hard.

One day, we realized we only had 15 grand in the bank. Our burn rate and our monthly expenses were $15,000 per month, so we had just one month of cash left and no deals under contract. Our offices at the time were just basically one room with a small wing for a conference table. By then, we had moved out of our first offices, as the sublet expired, and into a larger space of about 1,000 square feet at 226 East 54th Street. It was me, Paul, Ed Winslow, Jimmy Ventura, and Christie Moyle, our secretary. The five of us were very cozy in that space, and it was impossible to have a private conversation.

So, Paul and I needed to talk in private and went to my apartment, which was just a few blocks away. We couldn't talk about it in the office in front of everybody, so we walked to 300 East 59th Street and sat in my living room. "What the hell do we do now? Do we pay everything next month? Do we pay $5,000 a month for the next three months to pay the most important bills like the phone bill and pay to keep the lights on?" We really did say, "Do we go to Atlantic City and put it all on black?" And then we're like, "Hey, we have excellent credit and have a couple of credit cards each. Maybe we can go get more credit cards."

Having good credit served us well. For two days, we went to every bank to fill out credit card applications. We individually got a $2,000 card at this bank and a $3,000 card at that bank. By the time we were done, we had collectively amassed $60,000 in credit cards – four months of operating expenses! It was amazing that we got all the credit we did when we were applying for all these cards at the same time.

The credit cards helped in the short term, but we had to build our brokerage business, or we'd never be able to pay off the cards. We had to sell buildings. That meant we had to do all the basics. Notwithstanding the financial stress we were under, we never wavered from doing those basic things. We made calls every day, sent out our monthly mailings, did our quarterly Building Sales Journal newsletter, and attended networking events. All the blocking and tackling continued during those years – day after day, week after week, month after month!

~

Rod's Reflections:

Let me share some of the context of New York City in the late '80's. After getting my MBA from Duke, I had just started my first real job at Arthur Andersen's consulting division. My first consulting assignment was designing a trading system for Kleinwort Benson, a European stock brokerage firm. They were in the iconic Pan Am Building (now Met Life) on the 17th floor. I was there on October 19, 1987, when the stock market crashed by over 20 percent.

The following days, weeks, and months in the city were mostly filled with shock. One older man punched me as I was riding the subway to work just because I was reading the WSJ. He shouted at me, "It's all your fault – all you damn kids!" I witnessed the aftermath of someone jumping off a building. People were frantic. It felt as if the world as we knew it was coming to an end.

And this is where many businesses, especially brokerage businesses, fail. It's the chaos and the inability to find clarity in the whirlwind of the moment. Regardless of the economic cycles, Bob and Paul found a way; they were all in. As history tells us, there would be a few more "world-ending" events to come Bob's way, and yet he and his business would grow in the aftermath of each of these events.

~

CLIENT SUCCESS STORY: "I'M DYING, AND MY SISTER IS KILLING ME!"

One of the properties in my original territory was 1087 Second Avenue, a four-story mixed-use building on Second Avenue between 57th & 58th Streets. I had always spoken to the "owner," Harry Langer. There are actually several Harry Langers in New York City real estate, but this Harry Langer only owned one property – this one.

Harry was one of the first clients I cold called in 1984. I had called him every couple of months and sent him a piece of hard mail every month like clockwork. We had built up a great rapport and

Harry would almost always take my call or call me back. In retrospect, he was extraordinarily nice to me, given that I was just starting out and didn't know what I was doing. He always appreciated the market updates and information on the listings we were selling in his neighborhood. This was Harry's only building, and he always wanted to hear news about things that might impact the value of his most valuable asset.

Uncharacteristically, Harry hadn't called me back for a few months. One day in 1986, the phone rang and it was Harry. "Bob, sorry I haven't called you back, but I've had a heart attack and was in the hospital. I need to have surgery but don't have the money. I never told you this, but I own the property with my sister, Florence Kraus. I need to sell the building to get the money for my heart surgery, but my sister won't sell. We don't have any mortgage on the property, and my sister won't let me get one. I need the money desperately. Can you call her and try to convince her to sell?" Wow, what the heck??? I felt awful for this man.

I thought to myself, this is a strange situation. The sister won't help the brother when he needs heart surgery? I called her – she simply said, "I own half of the property, and I'm not selling." I explained to Florence that the property would probably be worth $1.2 - $1.3 million if it was sold. "I don't care. I am not selling," she said.

I called Harry and conveyed the conversation. He was practically crying. He couldn't mortgage his position because he needed Florence's approval.

Then I fell back on my broker licensing class and called Harry, "Harry, how do you and Florence own the property?" I asked. He said, "I don't know… what do you mean?". I told him that there are several different ways that two partners can own a building. He didn't know how they owned the property. I asked him to send me the deed. He did, and it was apparent that he and Florence owned the property as tenants-in-common. Remembering my licensing class, Harry could sell his 50% without Florence's approval. I called Florence and told her that Harry could sell his 50% without her and that if they sold together, they would each get more. She wouldn't budge.

Harry hired us to sell his 50% interest, and we immediately called the investors we knew. We had never sold a partial interest at that point and didn't know what to expect. I called another owner who had always been receptive to our calls and was interested right away. Benjamin Aryeh purchased Harry's 50% interest for $500,000.

The closing was scheduled to be way out on Long Island. Benjamin called me the day before, "Bob, there is no reason for you to go all the way out there. Come over to my office. I will pay your commission today". Benjamin paid our commission that day (the day before the closing), and I will never forget that!

He then started an avalanche of litigation with Florence and purchased her 50% interest for $400,000 two years later in a much better market. As they say, "Karma's a bitch".

Here are three key takeaways from this deal story for commercial real estate investors and brokers.

BK's Takeaways for Investors:

Understand Complex Ownership Structures

Understanding legal structures can give you strategic advantages. The different ways properties can be owned (tenants-in-common vs. other structures) can create opportunities. Benjamin Aryeh recognized the opportunity in buying a partial interest. He used litigation and market knowledge to acquire the entire building at a discount.

Build Relationships with Brokers

Benjamin Aryeh had previously been receptive to my calls, which led to this opportunity. He demonstrated professionalism by paying the commission early. He knew he was going to close and since the check would not have cleared by the next day, there was little downside here, but it was a fantastic and greatly appreciated gesture on his part. This helped build trust, which led to more opportunities from me as Benjamin became one of my first calls when an opportunity came up. The story shows how being reliable and professional with brokers can lead to unique opportunities.

Look for Distressed Situations

The urgent need for medical funds created a motivated seller. Family disputes and partner disagreements can create buying opportunities. Benjamin acquired both halves of the building at different times and different prices. The total acquisition cost was much lower than it would have been if he had to purchase the whole building at once, even after factoring in the legal fees involved.

When owners are in conflict, it can create opportunities for strategic acquisitions.

Rod's Lessons for Brokers

Build and Maintain Long-Term Relationships

Bob had consistently called Harry Langer every couple of months since 1984. He sent monthly hard mail updates without fail. The relationship was built on providing value through market updates and neighborhood information. When Harry finally needed help, he turned to Bob because of this established trust. This showcases how persistent, value-focused relationship-building can pay off years later.

Know Your Legal and Technical Fundamentals

Bob's knowledge of different property ownership structures (specifically tenants-in-common) was crucial. This technical knowledge helped him find a creative solution to what seemed like an impossible situation. He might have given up after Florence's initial refusal without this knowledge. The story demonstrates how fundamental knowledge can help brokers find solutions others might miss

Focus on Problem-Solving Over Pure Sales

Instead of just trying to sell the whole building, Bob listened to Harry's specific problem (needing money for surgery). The successful outcome came from solving Harry's problem rather than forcing a traditional sale. He investigated different angles when the initial approach didn't work. He thought creatively about partial interest sales. This problem-solving approach led to two commissions instead of none.

These takeaways align with the broader themes in this chapter about building long-term relationships, maintaining consistent communication, and focusing on creating value rather than just making quick deals. This story demonstrates how success in commercial real estate often comes from a combination of technical knowledge, relationship building, and creative problem-solving.

~

Rod's Reflections:

Creativity is born from curiosity and an expansion of basic business fundamentals. Bob sold half a building! His client was in desperate need of a solution, and Bob figured it out. Have you ever done that?

Oh, and Bob did that almost forty years ago. It was possible because he remembered the fundamental laws of property ownership. I wonder how many real property owners are reading this and running to their files to look at their property deeds. Are you in a bad partnership? Do you want an out – can you sell half of your asset, or whatever your percentage ownership is, without your partner's consent? Maybe you are a real estate broker reading this book and are now wondering what other solutions I haven't explored for my client.

~

When starting out, in a crisis, or in a very challenging market, you have to come up with novel and creative ways to make things happen and get deals done. We had to be resourceful when the universe threw us a curveball. Here's one example.

We wanted our presentation materials to stand out. At CB, we had fancy report covers and wanted the same for Massey Knakal. We picked a printer, and ordered a simple report cover: it was a black cover with a white knockout box and our green logo in the middle of the white box.

When they came back from the low-cost printer we chose, we quickly realized the printer didn't laminate them. We're picking up one of the covers, and suddenly, our thumbs and forefingers are all black from the ink coming off. We call up the printer and say, "What the hell did you give us?" He said, "Oh, you didn't tell me you wanted 'em varnished." I'm like, "Well, what the hell, did you think we wanted something that comes off on our hands?" You got to make new ones for us." The printer says, "No way." Then he suggested we perform a biologically impossible act.

We had no idea what to do. We just spent a lot of our limited cash, and we had hundreds of these things, and we didn't want to just throw them out. So, we went out and bought about ten cans of hairspray. We laid newspapers out on the floor, put the covers down, and sprayed the brochure covers with hairspray so the ink didn't come off on our fingers. Remarkably, it worked!

We made all kinds of adjustments to keep costs down. We used a different commercial printer for our first two quarterly newsletters and did them in two colors. When things slowed down, and we were being frugal, we did the next several newsletters in black and white on tabloid paper in our copy machine. Even with everything we did, it wasn't enough. By 1992, we had maxed out our credit cards, had little in the bank, and once again, no deals under contract. Here we go again.

Being in real estate in New York City, we have many clients with very deep pockets. One of those clients was a Forbes 400 investor worth about $450 million in the early 1990s. We had done a couple of deals with him, and he seemed to really like us. Surely, he would give us the $75,000 loan we were looking for.

We called to set up a meeting with him, and I vividly remember nervously walking up to his office. We discussed our circumstances with him and sheepishly asked him for a loan. He thought about it for a few seconds and said, "You boys know I really like you both, so I'll tell you what I will do. I will give you the $75,000, but I want 50% of the stock in your company." If you were in the room, you probably could have heard the air leaving our lungs. We thanked him and said we would consider it. Our chins were on our chests as we walked back to our offices, wondering what we were going to do.

We didn't want to give up half of the business. We had just one other place to go. Paul's step-father-in-law, Jack Holler, owned a mortgage brokerage business in New Jersey and did very well. We approached Jack, asked for the $75,000, and offered him 25% of the firm's stock.

Remarkably, Jack said he would give us the money but didn't want equity in the business. "Someday, you guys will be very successful and will regret having given me the equity," he said. Talk about a lucky break. It was the lifeline we needed. We were so appreciative of this extraordinary act of kindness that we named our Salesperson of the Year Award after Jack and gave it out in his honor each and every year thereafter! Whenever we gave out our annual awards, we explained who each of the folks were that the awards were named for. It was always very emotional to recount Jack's amazing kindness to us. I will never forget him or what he did for us.

So, we got $75,000 and were saved for the time being. But this is commercial real estate brokerage, and within a matter of months, that $75,000 loan from Jack Holler was spent on overhead. We had little in the bank, the needle was almost on E, and there was literally nowhere else to turn. We didn't know what we were going to do.

One of our listings was from Rosenthal and Rosenthal, who hired us to sell three buildings they had foreclosed on East 50th Street, between Second and Third Avenues. We marketed those buildings and relatively quickly put them under contract to the Shalom family, who owned several assets in our territory.

The deal was supposed to be a 90 to 120-day close. Paul and I didn't know how we would survive for those 90 to 120 days. Then, thirty days later, Steven Rosenthal called me up. I'm sitting at my desk. He's like, "Bob, where are you?" I said, "I'm in my office. What do you mean? Where am I?" He said, "Oh, we are closing 50th Street right now. The buyer decided to close early. Come on over and get your check." It was a $90,000 fee to us, so that's six months of operational expenses. I stood up and let out a scream, "Yes!"

I get up, and I put my jacket on. I'm running west, across 54th Street, to Third Avenue on my way to the closing, and Paul is just getting out of a cab, and I'm like, "Paul, Paul, 50th Street's closing! 50th Street's closing! I'm going to pick up the check." So literally, we hug each other, and we're jumping up and down on the southeast corner of 54th and Third. Anyone seeing this must have wondered what the heck was going on. We were so excited.

A couple of months later, we closed another deal. Then another. Then, the bank work created by the RTC started flowing in, and we were able to maintain traction. We started to make some good money again and could pay Jack back. But we never lost sight of the fact that Jack's loan and the Rosenthal deal saved us. But for those two things, Massey Knakal Realty Services never would have survived.

Interestingly, that deal was referred to us by Peter Hauspurgh, who owned Eastern Consolidated Properties, our number one competitor back then. They referred it to us because the buildings were mostly vacant, and Eastern was just focusing on income-producing assets at the time. Maybe Peter just thought it was a tough deal to make. Regardless of the reason, we were thrilled to have been referred that business. So that was a referral from another broker, and the deal saved our ass. We were always friendly with Peter, even though we owned competing firms. So perhaps there is a moral there – be nice to everyone. We probably would've been out of business if that deal didn't close.

Rod's Wrap-Up

The simple fact is there is no "right" time to pursue your dreams. The right time is when it's right for you. There is a rabbinic saying that "all beginnings are hard." That was true for Massey Knakal. And it was true for me and the Massimo Group.

Like Massey Knakal, the Massimo Group was born in one of our lifetime's most challenging economic times. In 1988, Massey Knakal had to deal with the S&L Crisis, and The Massimo Group, which really was just me and my wife then, was started during the Great Financial Crisis of 2008. Ironically, both crises were born from an irrational flush of funds to mortgages and a catalytic disruption that created an economic disaster.

Finally, Bob and Paul risked everything for their success. Maxing out credit cards, going to their family and or friends for loans, being humbled and taking on the basics of printing and mailing, and using hairspray to keep their report covers and their business dreams from fading away. Always remember, while there is no "right time to start," there is certainly no time to stop. Even when success starts to come your way, hard work and paying attention to the basics are still important.

BUILDING OUT THE COMPANY

When you start a business, things are slow at first. Revenues are almost flat, and profits may be non-existent. For companies that keep grinding on the basics, the hard work eventually begins to pay off, and the revenue and profit lines eventually turn up. The remarkable thing about Massey Knakal is that they survived for five years without making a profit while working on the basics and reinvesting every penny into the business. For them, the process of building out the company began when the market came back.

In this chapter, you'll learn what Bob and Paul did to create a unique culture. They developed a program to train new brokers their way. Even more important, they worked diligently to instill pride in every teammate. That pride and enhanced self-esteem propelled people to do better than their best and produced outsized results. You'll learn about how they reached a significant inflection point and how they decided what to do next. And you'll hear about the first of several offers to buy them out.

Let's pick up where the last chapter left off, with Bob and Paul literally dancing in the street.

~

The deal where we jumped up and down on the corner started to get us out of living on credit cards and the loan from Jack Holler. The deals started to flow after that, and the loan from our savior, Jack, was paid back, and over time, the credit card balances were reduced. From 1993, and 1994 through 2001, we grew to 21 people. The growth was steady as we became profitable and built out the company, but the growth only amounted to 17 people in 13 years.

It really was in 1993 and 1994 when we got a huge bump in activity because the banks loved our institutional approach to selling small buildings. This was a byproduct of the CB approach that was used for institutional sales. We simply adapted the institutional approach to the middle market, and the banks ate it up! We took that institutional approach of putting together glossy brochures and a full, comprehensive offering memorandum and applied it to small building sales. Nobody had ever done that for small buildings, and we were getting noticed for changing the way the market operated. Our results spoke for themselves. We did a lot of deals with the banks as sellers in those years, and that really gave us a big boost.

Profitability and Stoking the Fires of Growth

Massey Knakal was profitable for the first time in 1994, but Paul and I personally weren't making money. We were leaving money in the company and reinvesting every dollar in the business to make it grow. We took out what we needed, and we just kept the money in the business for more signs, more brochures, more newsletters, more hard mailings, more of everything to let the market know what we were up to. In later years, working with my coach, Rod Santomassimo, I learned that what we were doing were "market presence" initiatives. We were insanely focused on those activities. The more people knew who we were, the better it was for us. In recent years, I came around to articulating this as, "It's not who you know, it's who knows you." In the middle market world, this statement could not be more accurate.

We always had the philosophy, hey, if we have extra money lying around, let's invest it in the business rather than give it to each other. Let's go hire somebody else to relieve us of a task. Or let's do a capabilities brochure, an expanded newsletter, or something else that would make the business stand out. We kept doing that, kept pressing forward, and it worked like a charm. Soon, everyone knew us and what we did, and the snowball started rolling down the hill.

This was the actual start of the implementation of the territory system. Ultimately, we had folks in every neighborhood, or "territory" as we called them, in the whole city, but we started with one borough at a time. Manhattan was the first focus. We had a few people and were not yet covering all of Manhattan, but that was the goal. We were getting traction and knew we would come through this rough market and come out the other side with guns blazing. We decided to grow and fill up every territory in Manhattan. That was the objective, and that's what we did.

We're in the Information Business

We realized early on that we were really not in the real estate business but in the information business. In later years, we modified this to say, "we are in the information and relationship business". The real estate was simply the stuff the information was based on. To dominate the market, we had to have better quality information than anyone else, and by having experts in each neighborhood, we could easily develop better information than anyone else had. After all, New York City has hundreds of neighborhoods with over 176,000 investment properties. No one could know everything about all of them, but by having senior brokers focus on a concentrated neighborhood, they could know everything about every building and trend in their patch and provide real value to our clients. Providing real value to our clients, and putting them in positions to make more informed, and therefore, better decisions, is what this business is all about. We just figured out a better way to obtain that information and provide that value.

Creating a Culture with Servant Leadership

A big part of building out the company was creating the culture. The implementation of a servant leadership approach was number one. It was a servant leadership mentality in the true sense of the word. Most people talk nonsense about servant leadership. They talk about it, but they don't walk it. We walked the walk.

The servant leadership mentality has a lot to do with two things. Basically, it's building up the self-esteem of the people you work with by giving them constant feedback and guidance, showing you care about them. It is said the cruelest thing that can be done to someone is to not provide any feedback at all.

Second, servant leadership makes everybody feel that what they do is integral to the company's success. If you look at every major study that's been done on job satisfaction, the number one thing that always rates higher than money is feeling like what they're doing is important in directing the company toward its objectives.

So, we ensured that everybody in the firm, from the top producers down to the receptionists and the guys who stuffed the mail in the mailroom, knew what they were doing was meaningful and important to the company. This, more than anything else that we ever did, encouraged folks to do better than their best. To go the extra mile and to care so much about each and every thing they did.

We'd pull the receptionists aside and say, "Hey, you know what, guys? You're doing a great job. You're the first impression people have when they come to this office. And we love how you always greet them with a smile and offer them something to drink." After we talked with them, you should see how people were greeted when they walked through those doors. They were greeted as if they were the most important client in the world. That was great for the company, but it was also a reflection of them taking pride in what they were doing. Pride in your work is a great motivator.

We wanted to build them up. Make them feel great about themselves, support them, train them, encourage them, and let them know how well they're doing. And when somebody really feels like they're good, that gives them the ability to be great. And we wanted everyone to be great!

We also wanted them to enjoy working together and having the camaraderie of rowing in the same direction. We wanted everybody to like the folks they worked with and wanted their families to feel like part of the company as well.

Every year, we had a summer picnic at the Larchmont Yacht Club. All the spouses were invited, as were the kids. Even pets were invited. It was a real family thing; people talked about that event year-round until the next one.

We had social events and invited wives and husbands to every one of them. Look, the reality is that this business, at its core, is simple, but it is very hard at the same time. No matter how good you are, given the market's cyclicality, you are bound to have challenging times.

This business can grind you to a pulp if you don't have support at home. If you come home and your wife says, "Those guys you work with are a bunch of jerks," you're screwed. You're never going to make it. If your wife says, "You are working with good guys, and I understand when you come home, and I'd like to go out to dinner tonight, but you've got to work tonight. I totally get it." You have to have that support. So, as a business owner, you must have the spouse in your corner.

It was important that the wives understood, the husbands understood, and the kids understood that, hey, Massey Knakal is a good place. These are good people. They're going to do everything they can to help you and me. And maybe when the employees were doubting themselves, they got a little encouragement at home to hang in there and stick it out because the spouse liked and trusted us.

Take a simple thing like a holiday party. We had a black-tie party one year, and we had six dozen red roses, and we handed them out to all the wives as they came in. And you would be amazed; these women walked around holding that rose all night. We made them feel like we cared.

You make everybody feel special by just treating them well and, most importantly, remembering their name. On the way to all company events, I remember doing flashcards with my wife in the back of the car, memorizing all the spouses' names, kids' names, pets' names, etc. Remembering the wives' names was especially important. You greet the wife, call her by name, and hand her a rose. Suddenly, she knows, "Hey, I'm part of something here." And I think that that helped our culture significantly. Everyone was part of something bigger than themselves, and there was comfort in that.

Rod's Reflections:

During the 1990s, corporate culture was not as much discussed as it is today. Bob and Paul put in the effort to create a firm where people liked to work hard alongside people they liked, to make the firm successful. Bob and Paul did many things to help people understand what was important to them, like deep expertise and a quantitative orientation. They worked hard to instill their philosophy about the business. As Bob reminds everyone, "It's a marathon, not a sprint. Don't worry about today's deal. Worry about what's right for the client. It'll always come back to you." Training was one of the important ways they conveyed their cultural values to newcomers.

~

Training for Success

Here's how it usually is in the brokerage business, the approach is: here's a desk, here's a phone, go get 'em. The likelihood of success here is very small. We wanted to intensely train our folks. Why? Because it was in their interest, it was in the company's interest, and it was the right thing. And, most importantly, it was in the client's best interest.

The first training stage was called "Initial Success Training" (IST). When someone joined the firm as a producer, they were assigned a territory and had to "pass" IST before they were permitted to make a single phone call or speak to any potential client. Don't embarrass the firm by not knowing what you are talking about or being unable to add real value to a client.

During IST, the producer was tasked with becoming a market expert in their territory. This process included creating a list of every property within the geographic boundaries of the territory, obtaining and verifying the ownership and contact information for each of those properties, walking every street of the territory and taking photos of every property, using the contact information and photos to create "catalogs" for each block within the territory along with blank calling sheets on which to write down the notes from each interaction with the owner.

Once these catalogs were completed, we required a statistical analysis of the territory. This consisted of knowing who owned the most properties, the most square footage, and the most residential units. These lists helped prioritize prospecting and setting up meetings. We wanted to develop relationships with more prominent owners. The producers needed to know these lists cold. During the "checkout process," we would routinely ask, "Name the top five owners on each of those ownership lists." If you didn't know the answers, you were in trouble.

Then, we required the comparable sales analysis. A market expert can't be an expert without knowing the statistics. The producer needed to study every sale within the territory running back at least three full calendar years. How many properties were in the territory? How many of each type of building? How many sales were there in total each year? How many of each type of building? What was the turnover ratio? What was the average price per square foot of each type of property? What were the average cap rates for each type? What was the percentage of increase or decrease for each type? What was the dollar sales volume, and how did this fluctuate over the three years? What was the number of properties sold of each type, and how did this metric fluctuate over the three years? How did values fluctuate? Answer the most frequently asked question in the brokerage business: "How is the market?" with statistics rather than adjectives, and you put yourself in a position to be a trusted advisor, not just a broker. This is the position every broker strives to attain.

These first two training phases created a producer who knew more about their territory than any other broker in the market. No one else had the granular knowledge that our producers had, even though they hadn't even sold a single building yet. This created a rich database of "value" that could be conveyed to potential clients even though the producer had no sales track record yet. Adding value to a client creates an incentive for that client to take the call and talk to you. Talking to you allows you to develop a relationship and develop trust. Develop trust, and you have a client for life. But the training continues.

The third phase of initial success training covered how to "pitch" business. This included learning and understanding our "marketing process" and how to maximize the prices of the properties we were selling.

Our approach and value proposition was very simple: only sell buildings, only work for sellers, only work on exclusives, and focus on deals within the geographic territory. Understanding our marketing process and being able to articulate how each phase of marketing was going to be implemented gave the seller a "why" to hire us.

Our marketing program consisted of five phases:

1) Maximizing the property's benefits through marketing materials that highlighted what was compelling about the opportunity,
2) maximizing the exposure the asset would get in the marketplace,
3) creating a competitive bidding process,
4) the timetable for the typical transaction, and
5) how we remain accountable to the client throughout the sales process.

There was a whole chapter within the training manual for each of these phases. These were the main reasons why a seller would hire us and the main reason why we were able to achieve the highest prices in the market. We were agnostic as to who the buyer was. We created a level playing field for the buyer, got as many folks as possible involved in the process, got as many bids as possible, created a competitive bidding environment, and maximized the results.

The underlying premise of hiring Massey Knakal was to get the highest possible price. Our approach was not to make a deal. It was to implement a process that virtually guaranteed that every single market participant knew the property was for sale, a maximum number of offers were received, and the highest possible price was obtained. As a company that only represented sellers, the objectives here were unambiguous and transparent to everyone, especially sellers.

The double-edged sword of being a company that only represented sellers was that if we got high prices, we got more business – if we got low prices, we were out of business. We said this to potential clients, and it really resonated with them. Wouldn't you hire someone whose entire business revolves around getting the highest prices possible? If we didn't, we were out of business. How compelling for new clients!

The next phase of IST was learning how to underwrite property value and understanding the basics of putting a Broker's Opinion of Value together.

After completing this training, the producer had to "pitch" a panel of MK partners and "pass" this pitch in order to be authorized to get on the phone.

We gave them a hypothetical property to analyze, value, prepare a presentation book, and pitch the panel. If the producer passed, they could get on the phone and speak to potential clients. If they failed, they had one week to "clean up" their efforts and re-pitch the panel. If the producer failed, they would work daily with our director of training to sharpen their skills. If they failed twice, they were out. This rarely happened, but did on occasion.

After passing IST, all producers participated in "Continuing Success Training" (CST). CST was done via weekly training sessions and covered a wide array of training topics that allowed every firm member to sharpen their skills and become the best professional they could be. These sessions were generally led by our Director of Training, although there were several times when senior producers would guest lecture to provide insight into various aspects of the business. We also brought in guest lecturers from outside the company. These guest lecturers included Bob Cialdini (head of the psych department at the University of Arizona – the nation's top expert on persuasion), Bill Ury (Harvard professor who wrote *The Power of a Positive No.*), Richard Shell (Wharton professor who wrote *The Art of Woo*), Tom Donaldson (Wharton professor who is a leading authority on business ethics), and Richard Marcinko (the Navy SEAL who developed SEAL Team Six). These guest speakers provided invaluable lessons and instilled lasting motivation.

Our philosophy was that no matter how good you were at what you did, you could always do better. Up and down the line, you could indeed do better! Continued training was simply part of the job, and our goal was for everyone within the firm to "do better than your best!" Training would help you improve and so would observing how more experienced producers worked. This was one of the main reasons why Paul and I sat in the middle of the sea of cubicles and never in an office. We wanted to hear what they were saying, and we wanted them to hear what we were saying—no better training than that. After being required to sit in an office for six years at JLL, it's invigorating to once again be in the middle of the trading floor in a cube at BKREA.

CLIENT SUCCESS STORY: IT'S A MARATHON, NOT A SPRINT

One great example of "it's a marathon, not a sprint" was a deal that took eight years and eleven months from start to finish. It began in September 1992 when we were exclusively retained to sell the famous Club El Morocco building at 305 East 54th Street, where a who's who of celebrities partied in the 1950s and 1960s. It ended in August of 2001 with the second sale of the building within that timeframe. At the conclusion of this project, 13 different transactions allowed this assemblage to become a reality, having an aggregate consideration of approximately $30,350,000.

These transactions consisted of the sale of fee positions, the sale of transferable development rights, the relocation of tenants, the buyout of tenants, and a complicated property swap, which was the key to making the transaction happen.

For me, the most memorable part was tracking down an unresponsive owner who, no matter how many times I called her or sent her overnight packages, would never respond to me. She lived in Storrs, Connecticut. We knew we had the right address because she had signed for several FedEx packages we sent her. But she never took our calls, returned them, or acknowledged our existence in any way.

I decided the only thing to do was to drive up to Connecticut to see her. It was a risk, but we had nothing to lose. On the three-hour ride up there, I constantly thought about what might happen. Would she scream at me? Would she tell me to get the hell off her property? Would she have big dogs she would sic on me? Would she even be home?

I pulled into the driveway, and my mouth was dry. "What was I doing up here," I thought to myself. I must be out of my mind. When I approached the door, I didn't know what to expect, but I had a large bouquet of flowers (also, a handwritten note inside of a blank card in case she was not home). When she answered the door, she knew who I was immediately due to all the mail we had been sending her for years, which had my picture all over many of those pieces.

She invited me in for coffee and proceeded to tell me how much she hated all of the brokers who called her all the time (including me). Surprisingly, she was a very nice woman. She actually kept many of the mailings we sent her over the years with market info in a file in her desk. Talk about shelf-life. She never spoke to anyone because she never wanted to do anything.

We discussed the structure of a possible deal, which was something a developer could offer her that no one else could or would, which she said she would consider. I think she figured out that I wasn't some jackass trying to waste her time. Thank goodness for me.

After several months and several phone calls, when she would actually take my call, we finally made a deal with her. If the ice hadn't been broken this way, I'm unsure if the deal would have ever happened! We were very lucky, and a very risky move paid off.

Here are three key takeaways from this deal story for commercial real estate investors and brokers.

BK's Takeaways for Investors:

Complex Deals Create Opportunities

Complex deals can create value that wouldn't exist with simpler transactions. The final assemblage required 13 different transactions. Multiple transaction types were needed: fee positions, development rights, tenant matters, and property swaps. Being willing to work through complexity can unlock opportunities others might miss. The property swap was described as "the key to making the transaction happen."

Patience Creates Value

Sometimes the best returns come from being willing to wait. The nearly nine-year timeline allowed for proper assemblage. The primary building sold twice during this period as the pieces came together. Rushing the process would have likely resulted in less value creation. Complex assemblages often require patient capital and long-term vision.

Understanding Multiple Transaction Types

Understanding various transaction types gives investors more tools to work with. Success in this transaction required understanding various transaction structures: fee position sales, transferable development rights, tenant relocations and buyouts, and property swaps. Being versed in multiple transaction types creates more opportunities. The ability to structure creative deals can unlock value others miss.

Rod's Lessons for Brokers

Persistence and Creative Outreach

This shows how thinking creatively about contact methods can unlock opportunities. After years of unresponsive communication, Bob took the initiative to drive 3 hours to meet the owner in person. He came prepared with both flowers and a backup plan (handwritten note). The personal touch broke through where countless calls and FedEx packages had failed. Sometimes, the highest-value moves are also the most uncomfortable ones.

Long-Term Value Creation

The complexity and length of the deal demonstrates why brokers need to think beyond quick commissions. The deal took 8 years and 11 months to complete. It involved 13 different transactions totaling $30.35 million. Different types of deals were needed: fee positions, development rights, tenant relocations, buyouts, and property swaps. Success required maintaining focus and momentum over nearly a decade.

Building Trust Through Information

The owner realized Bob "wasn't some jackass trying to waste her time" because of his demonstrated expertise. The resistant owner had actually kept Bob's market information mailings in a file. This shows how consistently providing valuable market information creates credibility. Even when clients aren't responding, they may be paying attention. The face-to-face meeting worked partly because Bob had already established credibility through his mailings.

This success story exemplifies the chapter's broader themes about long-term relationship building, persistence, and the importance of maintaining a marathon mindset rather than looking for quick wins. Both brokers and investors who understand these principles are better positioned for sustained success in commercial real estate.

~

All the Manhattan Territories are Filled: What now?

From 1993 to 1999, we filled up all the Manhattan territories. This was Massey Knakal's first big inflection point. Looking back – how these inflection points were handled had profound impacts on our success. Now that all of the Manhattan territories are filled, what do we do?

There were two options. We could expand our service offerings and get into office leasing, store leasing, or mortgage brokerage or expand geographically to the outer boroughs to sell more buildings. This was before it was in vogue to be in the outer boroughs. Most Manhattan brokers thought their shoes would get dirty in the outer boroughs and avoided them. We decided that we didn't know anything about those other service lines. We knew how to sell buildings and would increase our geographical presence by going across the East River. The outer boroughs were calling our names, and we jumped in headfirst.

It was perfect for us. When you think of Queens, NY, you think of the six-story apartment buildings. There are thousands and thousands, tens of thousands of them, out there. You fly into the city, and you fly over these areas, and all we saw were places where we could put Massey Knakal "For Sale" signs.

We hired Tom Donovan, the brother of a trusted attorney friend of ours, to run our Queens operation in the first quarter of 1999. "Tommy D," as most refer to him, had zero real estate experience; however, he was a former beat cop in Queens. He knew every street and most of the owners. He was also a Marine and had an infectious personality that made him one of the most likable people we knew. Everyone loved him, and he had the exact work ethic we needed. He was the perfect person to help us open our first Queens office in the middle of 1999.

Once we'd filled the Manhattan territories, we opened an office in Queens. Instead of Paul and me and our secretary, we now had 21 employees. We were growing and getting the attention of our competition. This attention led to us receiving our first buyout offer.

The First Buyout Offer

In 2000, Marcus & Millichap approached us and wanted to buy us. They had been trying to enter the market for a long time, probably for over ten years. But they never got any traction as the folks they hired were not A players.

We had all of Manhattan covered, were selling a lot of buildings, and were growing in the outer boroughs, so we were a good target. Their first offer was $4 million, and they finally got up to six. We wanted seven million. In one of our meetings, I remember George Marcus saying, "Hey guys, look, we're making 25 percent returns on our internet stocks. Why are we going to pay you guys more?" And then the Dot Com bubble burst. No deal here. Onward and upward!

CLIENT SUCCESS STORY: YOU CAN'T MAKE THIS STUFF UP!

Back in 1996, the Catholic Archdiocese decided to sell a small property they owned at 128-130 East 58th Street. The building was previously the home of a church, which had vacated the property many years before. Normally, vacant churches that are not protected by "landmark status" make great properties to be occupied by user groups or as development sites.

This property was very well located on the south side of East 58th Street between Park and Lexington Avenues. The archdiocese had also sold its transferable development rights ("air rights") to an adjacent development site where the excavation of the site created foundation cracks in the subject property, which eroded its structural integrity. If the air rights hadn't been sold, the site would have made an attractive small development site. However, the lack of air rights prevented the site from being considered by developers, and the structural foundation cracks would make this a tough sale to a user group.

We were hired to sell the property and went on the hunt for a user who might have the sophistication to deal with the foundation problem. Along came what appeared to be the perfect buyer. A religious organization that was represented by a real estate investor/developer who was a member of the congregation. They could deal with the structural problems, renovate the property, and occupy it for their own use.

After a few weeks of back and forth, a deal was made to sell the site to this group, represented by the real estate guy, who we will refer to as "Mr. X." (His name has been changed to protect the guilty). The deal was made at $1,450,000, all cash, with a 10% deposit and a 90-day closing. The deposit was put up, and the contract was signed.

The representative at the archdiocese was David Brown, their head of real estate with whom we had closed many deals. Dave was pleased with the price and glad that another religious organization would occupy the property.

The day of the closing arrived, and we showed up at the offices of the archdiocese for the passing of the title. Dave was there, the attorneys for the buyer and seller, along with the title closer and Mr. X, who was a very well-known real estate investor who owned hundreds of properties in New York City. I was there with Jimmy Ventura, my childhood friend who was the second salesperson we ever hired at Massey Knakal. Jimmy and I were aware of Mr. X's reputation as a tough negotiator and had made Dave aware of that, a fact he was already aware of.

Mr. X walked into the closing room and, after exchanging pleasantries, sat down and said, "Dave, I have good news, and I have bad news. The good news is that I am ready to close today. The bad news is that I spoke to everyone in our congregation, and we could not come up with all of the money needed to close." The balance due at closing was $1,305,000. Mr. X reached into his pocket and pulls out a check for $1,005,000. "This is all we could come up with," he said.

He tried and tried to convince Dave to accept the lower amount, and after about half an hour, it was clear Dave was not going to accept the reduced amount. At this point, Jimmy and I are sweating through our shirts. We really wanted the deal to close and didn't want to let our client down.

Dave then asks Mr. X to leave. Mr. X then reaches into his pocket and pulls out another check for $100,000. "Okay, I was able to get the congregation to come up with $100,000 more. Please do a good deed and sell to us at the reduced price", he pleaded. Another 30 minutes go by as Mr. X tries to get Dave to take less, all to no avail. Dave holds firm. Jimmy and I continue to look at each other in amazement. Dave then asks Mr. X again to leave.

Mr. X then reaches into his pocket yet again and pulls out another check for $100,000. "Dave, this is the best we can do. Let's close!" he again pleaded. Dave walked over to the phone and called building security. "Please come right up and escort Mr. X out of the building." Dave then told Mr. X he was throwing him out of the building.

Mr. X continues to try to convince Dave to close at the lower price. As security enters the closing room, Mr. X pulls out the final $100,000 check with a sheepish look on his face.

The deal closed. Mr. X thought he was dealing with a seller he could push around. "Dave, you can't blame me for trying," was his parting message. You can't make this stuff up.

Here are three key takeaways from this deal story for commercial real estate investors and brokers.

BK's Takeaways for Investors:

Negotiation Tactics Have Consequences

Reputation in the market matters for future deals. Mr. X's staged check-pulling strategy ultimately didn't work and may have cost him in the long run. Aggressive negotiation tactics can damage professional relationships. The "You can't blame me for trying" attitude can burn bridges. Better to negotiate in good faith than risk damaging relationships. This approach can make you the broker's "buyer of last resort" where you only get to see opportunities after everyone has passed.

Understanding Property Constraints

The property had significant limitations: no development rights (air-rights sold) and structural issues from adjacent construction. These constraints affected property value and potential uses. Understanding physical and legal constraints is crucial for proper valuation.

Know Your Counterparty

Mr. X misread his counterparty (the archdiocese). He assumed he could push around a religious institution, but the archdiocese proved to be a sophisticated and firm negotiator. Dave Brown's firm stance showed institutional sellers can be tough negotiators. Assumptions about counterparties can lead to failed strategies.

Rod's Lessons for Brokers:

Know Your Players' Reputations

Background knowledge helps brokers protect their clients' interests. Bob and Jimmy were aware of Mr. X's reputation as a tough negotiator, so they proactively informed their client (Dave) about it. Understanding the players involved helps prepare clients for potential scenarios. This knowledge allowed them to anticipate potential negotiation tactics.

Professional Composure Under Pressure

Professional conduct during difficult situations preserves relationships. The brokers maintained their composure despite "sweating through their shirts." They let their client (Dave) handle the negotiation without interfering. They remained present and professional throughout the tense situation. They didn't try to pressure their client to accept a lower price.

Property Analysis and Positioning

The brokers understood the property's challenges: The air-rights had been sold, limiting development potential. Foundation cracks affected structural integrity. The result was a limited pool of potential buyers. So, they identified and targeted appropriate buyer groups (religious organizations) and recognized the need for a buyer with renovation/construction sophistication. Understanding limitations and opportunities helps target appropriate buyers.

This story illustrates how attempting to renegotiate at closing can backfire, the importance of understanding all parties' capabilities and motivations, and how maintaining professional integrity is crucial for long-term success in commercial real estate. It also shows how proper preparation and understanding of property constraints helps set realistic expectations for all parties involved.

~

Rod's Wrap-Up:

Bob and Paul developed their principles for building the business and stuck with them. These principles would become the pillars for the firm's growth and sustainability. Reflect on Bob and Paul's decision to keep profits in the company. Remember earlier when I shared how cash is king, especially in commercial real estate brokerage? Creating long-term success means employing discipline and sacrifice to put off what you would like today for what you really want tomorrow.

After working with thousands of CRE brokers and our sales team talking to thousands more, I know that most brokers can't wait to spend their commission dollars. However, cash management should be the first thing every broker trains their agent on when bringing on new team members. Bob was more focused on building a business instead of buying a new set of golf clubs. In fact, he didn't get off credit cards and "into the black" personally until 1999 – more than ten years of living off credit cards and having a net worth fluctuating between zero and a lot less than that!

Bob and Paul understood the value and importance of culture. They made everyone feel special, from the receptionist to their senior brokers to their employees, spouses, and kids. You may think this is easy when you are small, but this approach didn't change years later when Massey Knakal grew to over 250 employees.

The other key pillar was their focus on training. Not only their Initial Success Training but also their Continued Success Training. Massey Knakal invested in helping their employees and brokerage team get better, smarter, and more creative. Many organizations focus on onboarding new talent but ignore the fact that the greatest profits can be secured by increasing the skills of their most tenured team members. Retention is much easier than acquiring new talent, yet almost every firm takes their existing employees for granted. Bob and Paul never took anyone for granted, and their turnover of employees was minuscule by industry standards.

As you will see, Bob also had a "knack," if I may, for finding talent in the most unlikely places. That talent would ultimately lead Massey Knakal to the top of the mountain, and even today, it is scattered

across the leaders of New York commercial real estate investment sales brokerage.

9/11 AND THE AFTERMATH - BE PROACTIVE WHEN OTHERS PANIC

September 11, 2001 promised to be a fine day in New York City. The weather forecast was for a high of 78 degrees and clear skies, a lovely late summer day. As we know now, this day would be unlike any other in our lifetime.

At 6:00 AM, shortly before sunrise, the polls opened for the primary election. People were hurriedly making their way to work. You heard that familiar clanging sound as shops were rolling up their shutters. Everything looked like it would be a typical day in The Big Apple.

At 8:46, American Airlines Flight 11 crashed into floors 93 through 99 of the North Tower at the World Trade Center. The plane severed emergency stairwells, trapping hundreds above the 91st floor.

At 9:03, hijackers crashed United Airlines Flight 175 into floors 77 through 85 of the South Tower. Bob remembers looking out his office window and watching smoke pour out of the North Tower.

At 9:59, the South Tower collapsed.

Bridges and tunnels were closed to vehicular traffic. At 11:03, Mayor Giuliani ordered the evacuation of Lower Manhattan.

9/11 changed the world, the United States, and New York City. Times in the real estate market were already tough given the impact of the Russian Credit Crisis, the Dot.Com Bubble bursting, and the recession in the broader economy, but 9/11 threw the city's economy and commercial real estate even deeper into a slowdown.

The Chinese symbol for "crisis" is made up of two other symbols. One is 'danger," but the other is "opportunity." While many other people and firms panicked, Bob and his partner, Paul, ignored the danger and seized the opportunity. In this chapter, you'll learn what they did and how this risky move, perhaps more so than any other single decision, put Massey Knakal in position to dominate building sales brokerage in New York City when the market rebounded.

To tell that story, let's return to the morning of 9/11. Massey Knakal was implementing its growth strategy. The Queens office was open, and they were looking for people to run offices in the Bronx and Brooklyn.

~

I was sitting at my desk after arriving early that morning, as I typically did. My associates had also arrived early, and it was our habit to listen to Howard Stern's radio show until about 9 am, when I transitioned to smooth jazz on the radio. We were in our fourth office location at the time, at 18 East 41st Street just west of Madison Avenue, and were up on the 14th floor. Howard reported that "a small plane had flown into the World Trade Center." Everybody's like, "Oh my God, a small plane just flew into the Twin Towers." Then, about 30 minutes later, the reports were that it was a large plane, and a second large plane had struck the towers. The entire office hurried to the back of our space, which was facing south.

Between a maze of buildings, we could see the North Tower. We saw the smoke billowing out of it. Holy crap!

Within two hours, everybody in our office was kind of stunned, if not in shock. Reports quickly revealed that the event was a planned terrorist attack, and the city was shut down. Bridges and tunnels were closed, and the subway stopped running. Buses were abandoned in place. Our employees who were commuting from out of town could not get home.

We immediately went to the nearest deli and bought a ton of sandwiches, food, drinks, and all kinds of stuff. Who knew how long folks would have to use the office as "home?" Within hours, every hotel room was booked. Several of our team members hunkered in and had to sleep in the office that night. All the other people that lived in Manhattan were walking home.

After making sure everyone had what they needed, I headed home sometime after noon. The most surreal thing, and something I will never forget, was that walk to my apartment at 300 East 59th Street. The building was at the corner of 59th Street and Second Avenue, at the foot of Queensborough Bridge. I walked from our building on 41st Street over to Second Avenue and then started walking north on Second.

The scene on Second Avenue was shocking. It was a virtual sea of people, but the sea of people was utterly dead silent – eerily so. All you could hear were footsteps. There was no cell service; no one was talking. Even folks you could tell were together weren't speaking to each other. And every fourth or fifth person was completely covered in gray ash. And the smell of what was like rubber burning permeated the air and would for an entire week.

Everybody was heading to the Upper East Side or the bridge to make it over to Queens or points further east. All public modes of transportation were shut down, and roads were all closed, so cars were useless. People from Long Island were making their way to Queens to get picked up by a friend or relative.

I remember getting home, turning the TV on, and trying to comprehend what had just happened. Was anyone I knew killed or hurt? Would there be another attack? What do we do now? It was definitely a very, very challenging time.

We just didn't know what the heck was going on for a couple of weeks. We had some clients calling, saying, "Hey, I want to sell." One lady owned a property down in Chelsea. She said, "I'm moving out of the city; I have to get out of here. I'm selling. I'm moving to Iowa." Folks were scared.

Before that horrible day, there was a recession going on. A combination of everything the city and the broader economy was going through left many companies questioning their futures. Firms were downsizing and I just remember so many people being laid off. Great quality people from almost every industry were out of a job. Not just brokers but bankers, lawyers, accountants – no sector was safe.

Would Massey Knakal Hit the Pause Button on Growth?

It was probably a month later. Paul and I were contemplating what we were going to do relative to the growth plan we initiated in 1999 when we decided to open the Queens office and take over the outer boroughs. We had been on the hunt for someone to lead our next office in Brooklyn or the Bronx. Finding Tommy Donovan was the key to our opening Queens. We needed a leader and found a great one in Tommy D. Who would lead our next office?

And for the next office, the leader would also be a key. If we had found someone great for the Bronx, that would have been the next office. If it was someone great for Brooklyn, that's where we would have opened next. Would we keep on track with the growth plan, or do we hit the pause button?

I remember our conversation about the future coming around to the fact that we both believed unwaveringly in New York City. New Yorkers are tough, we said. We will bounce back from this. We want to grow, and hundreds of great-quality people are looking for jobs. What a great opportunity this is!

We planned to open additional offices in the boroughs. Those boroughs were filled with tens of thousands of investment properties that could be sold. Only about 16% of New York City's 176,000 investment properties (not including Staten Island) were in Manhattan. We had to get out there and needed lots of boots on the ground. This opportunity was staring us right in the face. We couldn't let it pass.

~

Rod's Reflections:

Bob's reasoning echoed classic investment advice from Nathan Rothschild to Warren Buffett: buy when everyone is selling. Downtimes are rich with bargains and opportunities. That's great general advice, and Bob and Paul supplemented it with some hard-headed analysis.

They were sure good times would return. All businesses have down times. And then they have good times. Then they have downtimes. It's a cycle. They believed times would be good again. They also had a lot of faith in the people of New York City. They were sure the city would bounce back.

They continued to maintain a strong market presence. Massey Knakal kept advertising. They kept sending out their monthly market updates and continued to publish their quarterly Building Sales Journal newsletter. That would have been enough for most companies. But Bob and Paul chose a bolder strategy.

They chose to take the dangerous and counterintuitive approach of adding people when everyone else seemed to be cutting back. They wanted to have the capacity to accelerate their expansion to the outer boroughs of New York City to take advantage of the inevitable return of a robust market.

They also took a novel approach to hiring.

~

Hiring Our Way

In the first quarter of 2002, we decided to hire a Director of Human Resources. Up until that time, Paul and I had been doing all of the recruiting and interviewing ourselves. If we were going to grow, and grow big, we needed help. This is one of the most important lessons over the course of our journey - delegate responsibilities to others in order to spend more time doing what you do best and delivers the most benefit to the company.

Gia LaMarca had worked for us in Queens since we opened that office. Tommy D. knew her and brought her in part-time to help stuffing envelopes for the mountain of mailings we were constantly doing. As the office was growing, so were her responsibilities. She was so good at everything she did, so naturally, we had her take on more. She was very young when we hired her and aspired to attend law school. However, she was becoming more and more valuable to us, and the Queens operation was gaining strong traction and growing quickly. Gia's job quickly became a full-time position.

So, needing a Director of HR which we discussed with our secretary, Christie Moyle. Christy said, "Oh, this girl Gia is fantastic. She's great. I love her." Seeing how quickly Gia picked up new tasks and how well she did at everything, we said, "Let's see if Gia wants to do it." And she's like, "I love you guys. I love working at this company. Sure, I'm happy to do it." And so, she transitioned from stuffing mail and doing administrative stuff in the Queens office into the HR role for the entire company and was awesome at it.

The first thing we did was to provide a vision for her to follow and some basic parameters of what we were looking for in candidates. We really didn't want to hire people who were brokers at other firms because they had likely developed bad habits, or at least habits we disagreed with.

Most brokerage companies allow their brokers to sell anything anywhere, anytime, anyplace. And you take someone who's been operating without any boundaries like that and ask them to work in a disciplined way and within a disciplined system, and it's just like the square peg in the round hole thing.

Our territory system required people who could use discipline well. We asked brokers to “Cultivate this box (their territory), know everything about this box from a building sales perspective, and if you get a lead from somebody you've done many deals with, but it happens to be in someone else's box, you are required to bring them in on that transaction. This was a far-out concept to most brokers who were freewheeling. If you didn't grow up in that environment, that's very abstract, and you're like, “Why the hell am I going to give that guy any money?”

The fact is this territory system was in the client’s best interest. It was also in the broker’s best interest. The client had someone on the transaction team who knew the area cold and could articulate to a buyer why they should pay more. And the broker didn’t have to schlep to another neighborhood, in maybe another borough, to show a building. The partner was already there, showing buildings all day anyway. It was a win-win, but the client's win was the most important. It’s always all about the client.

We also told Gia that regardless of how someone looks on paper, even if they have all the things we were looking for, such as competitive team sports, passion for the business, and exhibited excellence in their past work in a competitive environment, they could not be offered a job if she didn't like them. The test: after the interview, did she feel like she would like to go have lunch or a beer with that candidate? It was a great test and led to an unparalleled company culture. Dozens of employees were at every wedding. Twenty teammates were getting beach houses together for the summer. Friendships were formed that are strong and lasting even to this day. We were working with friends, not co-workers.

We found Tim King, who had spent his entire career in Brooklyn, to open that office. Timmy was great and was referred to as "The King of King's County." He did a masterful job growing the office in the largest boroughs. Of course, we had to keep selling buildings while we were hiring and expanding.

CLIENT SUCCESS STORY: THE LUCKY COIN: FROM COLD CALLS TO $179 MILLION

The company was growing quickly, but my focus remained on closing deals. Around this time, I closed my first $100 million-plus sale. It was a deal with industry legend Harry Macklowe, whom I started calling back in 1984 when I was at Coldwell Banker. There were two and a half pages of "left message," "left message," and "left message," and I could never get past Harry's secretary. Then, one night, I called his office at about seven o'clock. Harry's secretary had gone home for the day, and he answered the phone himself.

"Hey, Mr. Macklowe, this is Bob Knakal from Coldwell Banker."

"Yeah, yeah, I know who you are. You leave messages for me all the time and I have been getting all of your mailings. What do you want?"

That first conversation happened in early 1987. I kept calling him, talking about the market, offering him deals, and sending him our newsletter and other mailings every month. We did our first deal in 1997. Then, we did four more deals.

Then, one day, Harry called me. "Bob, come over to my office. I am going to make your year!"

After getting this message, what would you do? What did I do? I dropped what I was doing and ran over to Harry Macklowe's office.

It was 2003. The market was recovering from the recession in the early 2000s. Remember that Harry Macklowe was the whale that I cold called for two and one-half years. Between 1987 and 2003, I closed several deals with Harry and attained a solid reputation for getting great prices for apartment buildings in New York City.

I waited for 15 minutes in Harry's reception area, sweat streaming down my forehead due to the haste with which I hurried to his office. Finally, I was summoned in. "Bob, I have been watching what you have been doing, and I am very impressed. I need to sell my portfolio of 7 apartment buildings, and you will sell them for me," he said. I had never sold a deal for over $100 million in my career. These seven buildings were worth way more than $100 million. "I know this would be the biggest deal you have ever done, and that's why I know you will do everything possible to get me the best price possible for these buildings," he added. My heart was racing, and I wanted to scream!!

Richard Parkoff was an "old timer" who had been around forever and owned a massive portfolio of apartment buildings in New York City. Most of what he owned were not the most prime buildings in the city, but the tenants paid the rent, the cash flowed, and anyone in the world would want to own these buildings. To Richard's credit, he treated brokers better than most. Every December, a great holiday gift would arrive. Sometimes wine, sometimes crystal, and in 2003, it was a silver coin from Tiffany with "heads" on one side and "tails" on the other. The enclosed card read, "The next time we discuss a deal, I hope it comes up "heads" for me!".

Harry hired me exclusively. We brought the portfolio to market, and Richard was interested. Richard made a strong offer. He and his son Adam, read all 786 leases and signed a contract a few days later. Things moved fast in those days. The deal closed at $179 million. I was on top of the world. At the closing, Richard said, "I told you I wanted the coin to come up heads for me!"

The next day, I had the coin engraved at Tiffany with the inscription: "Macklowe to Parkoff 4/26/04 $179,000,000. I have carried that coin in my pocket every day since then.

Years later, in 2014 or '15, I was in Vegas for an ICSC (International Council of Shopping Centers) meeting and ran into Adam at the bar at Bartolotta's restaurant at the Wynn. Adam smiled when he saw me and said, "I bet you don't have the coin on you." I smiled back and pulled my good luck charm out of my pocket. We both laughed. I will never forget Harry, Richard, or Adam for providing me with this memory. And I will have this good luck charm in my pocket for the rest of my days.

Here are three key takeaways from this deal story for commercial real estate investors and brokers.

BK's Takeaways for Investors

Due Diligence is Critical

Richard Parkoff and his son read all 786 leases before signing the contract. This demonstrates the importance of thorough due diligence, even on large portfolio deals. Don't skip detailed analysis even when dealing with established sellers.

Build Relationships with Quality Brokers

Parkoff was known for treating brokers well (annual gifts and professional courtesy); this likely gave him better access to deal flow and market intelligence. Treating intermediaries with respect can provide competitive advantages.

Focus on Cash Flow Fundamentals

As I noted that Parkoff's buildings "weren't the most prime," but "the tenants paid the rent, the cash flowed." Focus on fundamental cash flow over trophy status. Reliable income often trumps prestige in real estate investing.

Rod's Lessons for Brokers

Persistence and Long-Term Relationship Building Pays Off
Bob Knakal spent 2.5 years just trying to get his first call with Macklowe (1984-1987). Even after making contact, closing their first deal took another 10 years (until 1997). The persistence in regular communication (calls, mailings, market updates) eventually led to multiple deals and ultimately, the $179M portfolio sale. Major relationships often take years to develop and require consistent nurturing.

Build Trust Through Track Record and Specialization
Macklowe specifically mentioned he had been "watching what you have been doing."
He chose Knakal precisely because it would be his biggest deal ever, knowing this would motivate maximum effort. The deal came because Knakal had established a solid reputation for getting great prices for apartment buildings in New York City. Developing expertise in a specific property type/market creates trust and opportunities.

Be Responsive and Prioritize Key Opportunities
When Macklowe called saying, "I'm going to make your year," Knakal immediately dropped everything and ran to his office. Bob knew the importance of being highly responsive to significant opportunities. Know when to drop everything for a potentially transformative opportunity.

These lessons demonstrate how success in commercial real estate often comes from persistence, relationship building, thorough analysis, and focusing on fundamentals rather than just seeking quick wins or trophy assets.

~

Rod's Wrap-Up

By mid-2003, the NY economy was starting to recover. The number of private sector jobs increased for the first time since 9/11. Massey Knakal had grown from 21 people to around 150. They had established divisions in Manhattan, Northern Manhattan, Queens, Brooklyn, and the Bronx.

This was done at the worst possible time from a market perspective. The sales volume bottomed out cyclically in 2003. When the market really started to recover in 2004, Massey Knakal was perfectly positioned to take advantage of the comeback. They had boots on the ground in every corner of the four boroughs.

Massey Knakal had a strategy in place when 9/11 hit. That was a plus. Their big bet was to double down on that strategy. If the market hadn't come back, it would have sunk them. It was a calculated risk, but it was still a risk, and they did it at a time when most wouldn't have. Plenty of research supports taking advantage of a downturn to improve the value of what you offer or increase your opportunities when the economy recovers. Bob and Paul did both.

Another risk was turning Gia into an HR Director. She didn't have the usual credentials for that kind of job. She turned out to be tremendous at the job, but it was impossible to know in advance if that would be the case.

My point? Lots of businesses know that finding the opportunity in a downturn is a good idea. But few turn that knowledge into action. And knowing isn't doing. You must be willing to take the risk and must believe in yourself.

Massey Knakal's response to 9/11 was part of their long game. They maintained an aggressive media presence, kept up their mailings without missing a beat, and maintained their focus on prospecting – understanding that no matter how difficult it can be, it is the most important activity a broker can implement.

Massey Knakal embraced the dangers of the post-9/11 crisis to seize opportunities to grow. In the next chapter, you'll learn how even more growth generated another buyout offer and the only serious disagreement in the 30 years of Bob and Paul's partnership.

IT WAS THE BEST OF TIMES.... UNTIL IT WASN'T

Like great marriages, great business partnerships have their rough spots. Bob and Paul had a remarkable partnership that started serendipitously without much thought and lasted for 30 years. They share a personal friendship that is still as strong as ever, many years after they sold the company. They went through so much together – doing all their early deals together and even painting their first two office spaces themselves. They took turns taking the trash out of their first three office spaces as the landlords did not provide cleaning services. They were joined at the hip and created and grew Massey Knakal together. In all that time, they only had one major disagreement. And it was a doozie!!

In this chapter, you'll learn how good times and an unsolicited buyout offer generated that disagreement. You'll discover the context and the roots of the disagreement. You'll learn how they resolved it and set themselves up to weather the Great Recession and obtain a substantially better offer in the future.

But I'm getting ahead of myself. Let's begin the chapter with the good times that followed the hard times post 9/11.

~

From 2000, sales volume dropped for three years in a row. The cyclical low was in 2003 at just 1.6% of the total stock of 27,649 buildings south of 96th Street, compared to the long-term average of 2.6%. In late 2003, you could feel things changing. Optimism was back in a big way; capital was being raised, and the folks who raised it wanted to deploy it. The market was sprinting out of the correction, and we were more than ready.

2004 --The Market Comes Back and We're Way Ahead

Everybody else is waking up saying, "Hey, the market's coming back. The outer boroughs look interesting and exciting; maybe we should take a look out there. Let's go hire some people". We had done that three years before that and were bullish on the outer boroughs long before they were hip and when other Manhattan brokers thought their shoes would get dirty if they crossed the river. And so, when other brokerage firms were coming up with a plan to enter the boroughs, we had boots on the ground all over New York City, and those producers had some time under their belts by the time things were heating up.

We had robust offices in Queens and Brooklyn, and every territory was filled by a productive salesperson. We ran Bronx and Northern Manhattan businesses out of the Manhattan office, and all three of those submarkets were also filled.

And here comes the market, thundering like a freight train, just as we hoped it would when we went on our hiring bender in late 2001 and early 2002. The market was on fire, and we were like 90 yards ahead of people in a hundred-yard dash. They had no chance, no chance at all. We were the top building sales firm in New York City by the number of buildings sold, and no one was going to come close to us. We knew we had a dominant position, and that felt great – like a giant adrenaline rush every time we walked into a pitch. We were on an incomparable roll. In some of those years, we sold 3X or

4X the number of properties as our closest competitor. And it felt so great for our little popcorn stand of a company to be clobbering the big national and global giants year after year for 14 years in a row.

CLIENT SUCCESS STORY: THE $28.8 MILLION QUESTION - ALWAYS CHECK THE MARKET

In late 2004, I was contacted by Andy Albstein, telling me that a client of his was selling a property, and he was not sure if they were getting a fair price. Andy is one of the top transactional attorneys in New York City and a great friend of mine for decades. Because he was so active and represented so many of my clients, I would always interact with Andy and was always pleased when I knew he was representing one of the principals in a transaction. Andy is also a very active networker, and I would frequently see him around town at various events.

Andy was representing a family that owned 25 Fifth Avenue, a classic pre-war elevatored apartment building of 15 stories and containing 90 apartments. The building had 105' of frontage on Fifth Avenue and 100' of depth on East 9th Street in the thriving Greenwich Village neighborhood.

We set up a meeting with the sellers, and they told us that they asked Andy to send out a contract to their managing agent, who had made an offer to purchase the property for $17.5 million. The family was a third-generation owner of the building, and the decision makers were not real estate people, so when they called

Andy and asked him to draft a contract, he said to them, "Don't do anything without checking with Bob Knakal first.".

Thankfully for them, they listened to Andy. In our meeting, I told the seller the price the managing agent offered was very low and, by any measure, they could get significantly more. They told me that the managing agent offered the property to three other buyers and had bids below the $17.5 that the managing agent was offering.

I explained that something didn't smell right, as 2004 was just at the beginning of a residential apartment building conversion trend that saw many rental buildings converted to condos. This dynamic was exerting significant upward pressure on apartment building values. The sellers were not aware of this recent trend. The family, impressed with our market knowledge, track record and Andy's stamp of approval, retained us to exclusively represent them in the sale.

We positioned the property as a condo conversion and marketed it to all the converter buyers. As we anticipated, the market response was overwhelming. In fact, we received 53 offers on the property and had three formal bidding rounds, including a final round in which sealed bids were submitted. In April of 2005, five months after meeting with me, the sale closed at $46.3 million. I was happy to provide some napkins for the managing agents to wipe the egg off their faces.

Here are three key takeaways from this deal story for commercial real estate investors and brokers.

BK's Takeaways for Investors

Market Knowledge is Critical

The family owners were unaware of the emerging condo conversion trend. That nearly cost them nearly $29M in value. Being unaware of current market dynamics can lead to significant undervaluation. The highest and best use can change with market trends. Regular market analysis helps capture maximum value.

Beware of Insider Deals

The managing agent's offer was severely below market value. Limited marketing to "three other buyers" resulted in artificially low prices, perhaps intentionally so. Insiders may have conflicts of interest when buying managed properties. Don't accept internal offers without testing the broader market. Limited exposure often leads to below-market pricing.

Seek Independent Professional Advice

The attorney's advice to "check with Bob Knakal first" earned the sellers millions. Third-party validation of pricing protected the sellers' interests. Professional advisors can identify opportunities owners might miss. Multiple professional opinions help ensure fair market value. Expert guidance can uncover hidden value (condo conversion potential).

Rod's Lessons for Brokers

Build Professional Networks

The opportunity came through an attorney's referral. Long-term relationships with other professionals generate business. Regular networking and maintaining professional relationships, pays off, and being known as a trusted advisor leads to referrals. Quality work leads to ongoing recommendations.

Create Competitive Marketing Processes
Bob generated 53 offers through broad marketing and conducted three formal bidding rounds, using sealed bids for the final round. Proper exposure revealed the true market value, and competitive bidding maximized price.

Add Value Through Market Intelligence
Bob identified the emerging condo conversion trend for the sellers and positioned the property for its highest and best use. He targeted the right buyer pool (converter buyers). And he understood the market dynamics affecting value. These combined to deliver crucial market insight that dramatically increased value.

This story demonstrates how proper market knowledge, broad marketing exposure, and professional advice can dramatically affect sale outcomes. The nearly $29 million difference between the internal offer ($17.5M) and the final sale price ($46.3M) underscores the importance of investors aligning with market experts like Bob.

~

Rod's Reflections:

This was when it became obvious to everyone in the company, and even everyone outside the company, that Massey Knakal was something special. And, as I constantly remind my coaching clients, you must learn the fundamentals and have the discipline to implement those fundamentals over and over again. That's exactly what Massey Knakal had been doing for about 14 years. They trained brokers on the fundamentals, implemented a servant leadership management style, and maniacally trained the troops. They never lost sight of the fact that even the slightest victory should be celebrated, and building the self-esteem of every team member, from top to bottom, would get the most out of them.

Bob and Paul took some big risks. Their hiring spree in the early 2000s could have sunk the firm if the market hadn't come back. They believed and put their money, pretty much all of it, where their mouths were. But they put their heads down and continued to do those fundamental things and made sure everyone did them and did them over and over and over again.

~

2006 and 2007 – The Best of Times

So, when volume really started to crank in 06 and 07, it was a glorious time. No doubt about it. I mean, we were cooking on all cylinders. Everyone was making a ton of money. Our market presence was outrageous. Our Building Sales Journal newsletter grew to 32 pages. We were selling a dozen $5,000 quarter-page ads in the newsletter to a variety of people who wanted to reach our client base. The circulation was over 330,000 per issue, and we probably had 250 people at Massey Knakal.

It was a glorious time in the market for everyone. Market conditions could not have been any better, and everyone was growing, hiring, thriving, and trying to figure out the next best way to grow.

Another Buyout Offer

In March of 2007, Mary Ann Tighe of CBRE, who's one of the top office leasing brokers in the United States and a good friend, calls up and says, "Hey, Brett White's in town, and we'd like to talk to you. Can you come on over?" Brett was the CEO of CBRE at the time. So, I go over and meet with Mary Ann and Brett, and they're like, hey, we're doing great. We got a lot of excess cash, and we'd like to buy you guys. I wasn't all that surprised.

We had been approached occasionally before, but we politely rebuffed the advances (with the exception of the flirtatious affair we had with Marcus & Millichap in 2000). But this time was different. We knew the numbers in 2004, 2005, 2006, and year to date in 2007 were steadily improving. I thought to myself, "How long can this last?" Each time sales volumes rose for three years in a row, the next year saw a drop (1984-1986, 1996-1998). It was also curious that even though sales volumes declined during the recession in the early 2000s, values didn't fall in a single year.

I decided to have CBRE sign a Confidential Agreement and give them some of our numbers—all without telling Paul, whom I knew would not want to speak seriously with CBRE or anyone. That was a BIG mistake on my part. Sure, everything came out right in the end, but I would not do that to another partner of mine ever again.

I gave the CBRE folks our financials, and they said, "Okay, let us think about it. We'll come back to you." Over the next several weeks, they had many questions, which I answered, and we had another couple of meetings, all without Paul.

MaryAnn calls me and says, "Bob, Brett is coming back to town, and we want to meet with you and Paul. We are ready to make an offer!"

Gulp!!

I have to go in and tell my partner and my best friend that I have been speaking to CBRE for months without his knowledge, and they want to make a bid.

Paul was angry– and I can't say I blame him. After all, what was I doing speaking to them on my own?

I set up the meeting, and we met with Brett and Mary Ann. I so vividly remember Brett standing up, leaning against the wall, staring out the glass walls, seemingly thinking about something else, telling us that CBRE had "$220 million of free cash sitting on our balance sheet; it's growing every month, and we'd like to give you guys some of it."

I was looking directly at Brett and could see Paul out of my peripheral vision. He did what Paul would so often do when he was mad: he sat there and didn't say a word. The "Massey Stare" kicked in, and those cold daggers were aimed right at me.

Brett said, "We want to buy you guys, and we'll give you $50 million. I was excited.. Paul still didn't say a word. I simply said, "We'll go back and think about it and get back to you." Paul politely said goodbye and didn't say a word on the elevator ride down.

When we got out of the building, he let me have it. As I sit here writing this, I'm getting very emotional. I really hurt him, and for that, I am truly sorry. I messed up. How could I have done that? We weren't going to have a productive conversation on that agonizingly long three block walk, so I peeled off to get a shoeshine. I had that feeling like you do when you don't really know what to do or what to say. Even though there was a city full of people around me, I felt completely and utterly alone.

A few hours later, I asked Paul to join me in the conference room. We talked about what had happened, the offer, and what we were going to do. Paul said, "Look, we can grow this thing more. We take it to the next level. I have no interest in selling." I'm like, "Paul, it's 50 million bucks. We were ready to sell for $7 million, seven years ago. We started this thing with nothing, and that's a lot of money. I want to take it." And he's like, "Bob, Bob, I don't want to sell. We can keep going." I'm like, "This is a crazy market. This is crazy. Look at what's going on. This is not gonna last."

Of course, I had no way of knowing that the Great Recession of 2008 was right around the corner, but I did sense that we were nearing the top of the cycle and that there was no better time to sell than now.

We were at an impasse for the first time in the 23 years we had been partners and friends. The more I tried to push, the more he dug in. We told CBRE "Thanks, but no thanks!"

A Great Partnership Under Strain

I told myself that he was just upset because I held those meetings for months without him, but I think he truly loved the company so much that he just couldn't let go. You see, we changed over the years.

We did everything together for the first ten years or so, but as the company grew, we began to gravitate toward different aspects of the business. I was Mr. Outside, speaking at conferences, going on TV, networking like a madman, and selling, selling, selling. Paul was Mr. Inside, running the company, managing people, putting out fires, and managing our enormous growth. If we sold, I could still do what I was doing at CBRE; Paul would probably have his responsibilities "adjusted."

The only solution we could think of was for Paul to buy me out. We talked about it a bit, but the thought of us "divorcing" was an extraordinarily difficult one for me. I vividly remember sitting in his cubicle with him, tears in my eyes, telling him that I would agree to him buying me out. It really was like a couple divorcing, but not a couple who hated each other, but rather a couple who loved each other but just realized, for some reason, there was just no future for them together. It was the most difficult situation I have ever had to deal with professionally. It's a painful memory.

For weeks, we negotiated a term sheet. Naturally, our partners and teammates suffered during this time. Everyone knew what was going on. We were making them choose between living with mom or dad, and we both felt terrible putting them in that situation. Our negotiations dragged on, and by the time we had arrived at terms we both agreed to, the market had started to turn a bit, and Paul was unable to come up with the money to buy my interest.

By early 2008, the market was getting bad. Given what was happening in the broader market, Paul's buyout offer was not feasible. Paul and I realized that the only solution was to suck it up, reconcile, and move forward. At our annual awards ceremony, which was held in the Brooklyn office that year, Paul and I announced to everyone that we were sticking together and Massey Knakal would not be sold, and the partners would move forward – together.

The Great Recession – Hard Times Return

2008 and 2009 were awful. Bear Stearns, Lehman Brothers, and AIG failed. The banking system appeared to be on the brink of collapse. The Great Recession took hold. We had to cut 25 percent of our people, and it ripped our guts out.

In 2004-2006, we were invincible. Just two years later, in 2008, we couldn't zero out our $2 million revolving credit line for 30 days as was an annual requirement, and we had to make a deal with our bank. Thankfully, they were great to work with and gave us a break. In 2009, if we had to sell Massey Knakal for some reason, we would have been lucky to get a few million. But we kept fighting, kept believing, kept doing the fundamentals. Positive thinking is an extraordinarily powerful thing, and while it wasn't easy, we remained positive. I never once said, "I told you so". By 2009, Paul and I were totally aligned once again. Our strong friendship and our bond, which lives to this day, got us through my misguided error.

One good thing that came out of the debacle of the attempted sale was a kind of clarity about how we'd approach a buyout in the future. It became clear to us that when we did sell, we would be on at least 5-year employment contracts with the buyer. We decided, back in 2008, that because Paul would be turning 55 in February of 2015 so 2014 might be a good time to sell as the perception would be that those employment contracts would have more value if we were in our fifties than if we were in our eighties. So, we decided to sell in 2014 if the market wasn't in a bad spot. As fate would have it, and completely unbeknownst to us at the time, 2014 would be the perfect time to sell.

Rod's Wrap-Up

Can you imagine a point in your life where someone offers you $50 million dollars for your business, and your partner says no? And worse, within 12 months, the market crashes, and your business is worth a small fraction of that original offer? Think about that. How many partners would move forward with total resentment and always question, "What if?"

But that wasn't what Paul and Bob did. They were partners and decided to use this major conflict as a call to action. That action was a dissolution plan. Do you have a dissolution plan? Do you know what "your number" is? You know how your company and employees, or even small team members, would be taken care of should you sell or should you pass.

At Massimo, every COO I have had (I have had three in 15 years) must write a "what if" document outlining what they would do if I fell ill or worse. I need to know how the company will move forward. Likewise, my partner (my wife) and I have our own internal plan, and yes, even strike price, for when we would sell Massimo. But, as Paul Massey told Bob about Massey Knakal in 2007, I know we can take Massimo to a whole 'nother level.

This short chapter covers a lot of lessons in a short period of time. Here are just a few.

Bob and Paul took a risk by hiring and expanding while other firms were pulling back after 9/11. That was risky, but there was a big payoff. When the markets came back, Massey Knakal surged to the front of the pack. As Bob said, "We were like 90 yards ahead of people in a hundred-yard dash."

Success was built on more than one bold stroke and a little luck. Bob and Paul built a strong culture with strong values. They developed basic systems that their people could follow. Then, they hired people who would be comfortable in their system, trained them extensively, held them accountable for results, and built up their self-esteem.

One more thing about that success: It was built on doing the basics with unremitting diligence. They did the right things. Prospecting was critical, as was market presence and delivering value to their clients. We talk a lot about how important hard work is, but hard work on the wrong things takes you in the wrong direction. Do the basics, do them well, and keep doing them, as Bob says, "over and over and over again."

Bob and Paul had an incredible partnership. It might be the best one I've seen in all my years in business, and it has lasted for 30 years. As Bob said in an earlier chapter, they trusted each other, were fair, and really cared about each other. They both had the same work ethic and thought about the business in the same way. But as good as their partnership was, they went through a rough patch. That's going to happen.

Finally, there's a lesson that it seems we have to relearn again and again. The commercial real estate business, and every business, is cyclical. There are good times followed by bad times followed by good times. 9/11 was a bad time, but one of the best times followed it. Those good times were temporary, and they were followed by, you guessed it, bad times. In this case, the bad times were the Great Recession.

In the next chapter, you'll see just how hard it was for Massey Knakal and learn some important lessons about how you can respond when times get really hard.

IT WAS THE WORST OF TIMES

Bob and Paul reconciled, but as Bob noted, the market was starting to crack. The Great Financial Crisis had begun, and that glorious period from 2004 to 2007 was in the rearview mirror.

Let me set the stage for you. Whether you call it The Great Financial Crisis (GFC) or The Great Recession, it was the deepest and most damaging downturn since the Great Depression. Ultimately, it affected the entire world.

The recession officially began in December 2007. In 2008, Bear Stearns and then Lehman Brothers failed. The government intervened, taking control of Fannie Mae and Freddie Mac and starting the Troubled Asset Relief Program (TARP) to save the US banking industry.

Banks became more cautious and reduced their lending. Employers in New York City laid off more than 100,000 workers and cut costs wherever they could. People were running around New York City opening bank accounts with no more than $250,000, so FDIC insurance would be applicable if their bank failed.

In New York, commercial real estate sales dropped 61 percent as prices dropped everywhere. Manhattan condominium sales volume fell 30 percent in 2009. Midtown Class A office vacancy rate rose above 12 percent.

Commercial Real Estate is cyclic, so you can expect downturns, but there's no "one" strategy that will work for every firm in every recession. Context matters. That's the focus of this chapter.

We've seen how, after 9/11, Bob and Paul doubled down on their growth plan and committed to hiring many people. This seemed counterintuitive at the time, but they were believers—believers in the future of the city they loved so much. That strategy, risky as it was, paid off big time. However, the downturn that was the Great Financial Crisis posed a very different challenge for the company.

Going All-In

After 9/11, we had just 21 people, and growth in the early years was slow and steady. Our monthly burn rate was not high by design. After all, we had no outside investors in the company – everything was self-funded, so we always needed to keep an eye on operating costs. But after our hiring spree, which was done to take advantage of the opportunity we saw, that conservative approach was out the window. We were going all-in, and we were going big.

The Advisory Board

We made hundreds of mistakes when we were growing Massey Knakal. Those mistakes were made mostly because our approach to doing things was trial and error. What were we thinking? This is one of my biggest regrets because we could have saved a ton of time had we simply asked people with more experience for their advice.

In 2007, we formed an Advisory Board. The folks we called on were all our friends, and each graciously agreed to join our Advisory Board and meet with us quarterly to help us grow the firm. The people we originally had on the advisory board were Ric Clark, the president of Brookfield Properties, a large public company that owned millions of square feet of buildings in New York City and around the world, Stephen Siegel, the chairman of global brokerage at CBRE, the world's largest brokerage company, Michael McVicker, the head of the trading desk at Morgan Stanley, Paul Salvatore, the head of the labor law practice at Proskauer Rose, one of the largest law firms in the world and our labor lawyers at Massey Knakal, John Fowler, one of the named partners in Holliday, Fenoglio, Fowler (HFF), Ofer Yardeni, the CEO of Stonehenge Partners, the owner of thousands of multifamily units in New York City and a great client of ours.

The GFC Hits Hard

Now, we had about 250 people. Our burn rate was big, and our payroll was over $5 million per year. So, when the GFC came, we really had to figure out how to survive. We had to make cuts and make them fast! And that's what we did. It was one of the toughest things we ever had to do. We had to cut our staff by 25%.

Our Advisory Board members urged us to make the cuts quickly. Because of them, we made the cuts sooner than we would have, which may have saved Massey Knakal. Cutting staff is hard, and without the push from the Board, I doubt we would have cut soon enough.

The most difficult thing was realizing the impact this was having on people's lives. They had spouses and children and relied on us for their livelihoods. It was gut-wrenching and probably the most significant contributing factor to my not wanting to start another business after the C&W years concluded.

If you have ever had to tell someone they were losing their job, and they break down and start to cry in front of you, you know exactly what I mean. Some took it okay, others not so much. A couple just got up and walked out of the room without uttering a word. It pains me to remember those meetings and, all these years later, recalling those times still stings as if they just happened. Business is not cold and cutthroat as some might lead you to believe. These are real lives, real feelings, real emotions, and the way we treat people cannot be taken lightly. But cut we did because we had no choice if we were going to survive. This was probably my darkest period within the 26 years of Massey Knakal's life.

Getting through the GFC was ugly, really ugly. And as I stated above, it was very emotionally challenging for me. We had to let 60, 65 people go, which was brutal, totally brutal. It ground me up because those folks were really good people who didn't deserve this fate. And because of the way we ran the company, we knew everyone's spouse's name, the kids' names, even the pet's names. This was like kicking family members out of the house. Paul did most of the firings; I just couldn't do it anymore.

We had a $2 million revolving credit line that helped us smooth things out, given the volatility of cash flow in the brokerage business. The term on those revolving credit lines is that you have to maintain a zero balance for a 30-day period every year to keep it active. It is not perpetual debt. And we didn't have the money to zero it out—not even close.

It was a far cry from our $60,000 credit card debt in the early nineties. That credit was four months of burn back then. Today, we had a $2 million credit line, and our monthly burn rate was almost $3 million! Our line was maxed out, and we couldn't zero it out. We had to go to the bank. We actually switched banks to get that credit line because Chase, the bank we had been with since back in the Coldwell Banker days (Chemical Bank back then), wouldn't increase our $1.2 million revolving credit line to the $2 million we wanted. So, we went to Citibank, which wanted all of our banking business and was willing to give us the $2 million line to get it. So, we made a deal with the bank to make payments over time to zero it out. Another lucky break for us!

At the time, I was relatively newly married to my wife, Cynthia. Our daughter, Sophie, was a year old. I'm working my tail off, pretty much around the clock, other than the gym and church, because we need to keep the company alive and make it through this. And it was hard – this perpetual grind that was taking me away from my family. But I had no choice.

Rod's Reflections:

Yes, it was seemingly the worst of times. When the GFC hit, I was a senior executive for Sperry Van Ness and "commuting" from my home in North Carolina to California every week. But like Massey Knakal, Sperry Van Ness (now SVN) had to lay off people. Every company had to lay off people. It was estimated that over 20% of the commercial real estate brokers left the industry during the GFC. and I found myself unemployed with no jobs to be found—especially jobs in commercial real estate.

While the Great Financial Crisis took a toll on Bob, Massey Knakal survived. Sometimes, the best possible outcome is staying alive so you're ready to go when times get good again. Despite everything that was going on, Bob continued to do what he did best: sell buildings.

I too, managed to survive. In fact, being laid off allowed me to reflect and define how I wanted my future to move forward. One thing I knew was that I was tired of working for "the man." Hell, I was never good at not being the boss. Funny, neither was Bob.

At this time I was 45, and Bob was 46, and little did we know that our paths would cross, for the very first time, in the next year.

CLIENT SUCCESS STORY: THE BIRTH OF THE VIRGIN HOTEL

In land assemblage, the whole is usually worth more than the sum of its parts. The assemblage that led to the site for the Virgin Hotel at 1225 Broadway was extraordinarily complex. Due to an unusually shaped property and different zoning districts, the sum of the parts were worth significantly more than the individual parts. Suggesting a tax lot sub-division and a joint venture development strategy, leaving one of the obstructionist sellers with a retail condo interest, were the keys to maximizing value for my client.

In early 2006, with the development market in full stride and the broader market surging, a long-time Massey Knakal client decided to sell 1227 Broadway and 846 Avenue of the Americas. Two adjacent properties comprised the entire southerly blockfront of West 30th St. between Avenue of the Americas and Broadway. The two properties formed a very unusual triangular-shaped site with just 15' of frontage on Broadway.

Given its shape, it would be very difficult to find a developer to construct a building on the site, given contextual requirements, particularly given that the properties were in two different zoning districts: part of the site was residential, and part was commercial.

I had sold several properties for Howard Waxman and Mike Feirstein, the owners of this triangular parcel. They hired me exclusively to sell this one.

The total buildable footage of the two properties was about 120,000 square feet. We anticipated a price of about $400 per buildable square foot for the 69,000 square feet, which was in the residential zone, and about $300 per buildable square foot for the 50,600 commercial square feet.

I approached the owner of the adjacent properties at 1205 and 1225 Broadway. These properties were owned by Mocal

Enterprises, which was owned by another long-time client of mine, Cal Haddad.

Cal's buildings were occupied by short-term office tenants (one-year maximum term) and short-term retail tenants (three-year maximum term). I suggested to Cal that by putting the properties on the market, he could take advantage of the strong development market and, with the potential to join forces with the neighbor to the north, deliver the entire block front on Broadway between 29th and 30th Streets to a developer.

Cal loved the strategy and hired me. A couple of months after going to market with both offerings (two properties each), the owners of the triangular parcels decided to withdraw their properties from the market.

However, the marketing of 1205 and 1225 was progressing well, so Cal decided to stay the course. The marketing program produced a buyer willing to wait for tenancies to expire. A contract was signed in mid-2007 for about $92 million.

The buyer was willing to close quickly, but Cal requested a nine-month closing period to provide more flexibility to effectuate a 1031 tax-free exchange. The contract price was $368 per buildable square foot, an enormous price for an M-zoned piece of land at the time. The buyer put up a $9.2 million non-refundable deposit, which he agreed to release from escrow at the seller's request.

During the negotiations, Cal asked the buyer for proof of funds. We were in a conference room at the buyer's office. He called out to his assistant "Bring me my bank statement from last month."

Within two minutes, the assistant walked into the conference room with a bank statement showing $173 million in cash in a checking account! I have learned over the years that the folks who have money are happy to prove it, and those who don't have the money will give you every excuse in the book as to why they can't demonstrate it.

A couple of months after Cal's contract was signed, the contract vendee called me to ask about Howard and Mike's adjacent properties. "Bob, can you shake those loose?" I called them, and they had no interest in selling. I explained that this was the one chance they had to get a fair price for the 1227 Broadway parcel, given its small size but profound impact on the blockfront. They still said "no."

Howard and Mike called two weeks later to say they had changed their minds and would now consider a sale. Negotiations began and the contract vendee was aggressively pursuing those adjacent parcels. However, the closing date was rapidly approaching on Cal's parcels and the contract vendee asked Cal for an extension of the closing date for 90 days. Given Cal's trepidations about the vendee (notwithstanding the proof of funds provided), he declined to extend the closing. "This is what I was concerned about from the beginning," he exclaimed.

The proposed closing date came and went, and the vendee defaulted, losing the $9.2 million deposit, and sued Cal for the return of the deposit. This unsuccessful attempt caused an almost two-year delay in the sales process. After Cal won the litigation, he decided to sit on the asset until the market improved.

By early 2011, the market was improving. Cal retained me again to sell the buildings.

Being a glutton for punishment, I called my buddies Howard and Mike again to see if they would be interested in joining the sales process. They were not ready to go back to the market at that time.

The development market had started to recover, and interest in Cal's properties was very significant. Most of the prospects who were interested in Cal's properties also wanted Howard and Mike's properties.

While those properties were not on the market, most prospects made unsolicited offers to Howard and Mike through me. None of these buyers allocated a significant enough value to those properties to compel the partners to sell them.

The Lam Group was identified as the top bidder for Cal's site, and they wanted the adjacent properties. They signed a contract on Cal's parcels in the spring of 2011. That sale, now at $71.9 million ($287 per buildable square foot), closed in August of 2011.

Now that Cal's properties were sold, Howard and Mike were somewhat at the mercy of Lam as they controlled the balance of the blockfront on Broadway. As such, they were able to attribute the highest value to the adjacent property potentially. Unfortunately, Lam was not willing to pay an acceptable price for the properties because they were going to build a hotel on the site. The value of Howard and Mike's properties was significantly higher because of the residential zoning that existed on the western part of their site.

Lam had no interest in any of the residential air rights as they were only hotel developers.

Feeling that they may have missed an opportunity, Howard and Mike retained me again, and I had to figure out how to deal with the awkward shape of the combined lots.

I suggested to Howard and Mike that they subdivide their middle lot along the zoning district boundary such that the eastern part of the site, which was entirely in the commercial district, could be sold to Lam so he could have the entire blockfront and the most valuable piece of Howard and Mike's properties could be sold at a higher price.

They loved the idea. We floated this past Lam, and they loved the idea as well.

We negotiated an acceptable contract between the parties to sell the subdivided lots to Lam for $16,000,000, or $316 per buildable square foot, a higher price per buildable square foot than Lam paid for Cal's properties. This contract was contingent upon completing the sub-division. This transaction closed in November 2012.

Now, the question was what to do with the balance of Howard and Mike's site. This property was now put on the market at an asking price of $400 per buildable square foot, or $27,600,000. After months of marketing and negotiating with several prospects and loads of back and forth, the property was taken off the market and then put back on. We eventually sold the site to Ken Horn at Alchemy Partners, and they built a condo on the site. We did a creative deal structure that allowed a reluctant Howard to stay in the deal and wound up with a two-story retail condo on a tax-efficient basis.

So, over many years and a volatile market with an up, a down, and a backup, the Virgin Hotel site was born.

Here are three key takeaways from this deal story for commercial real estate investors and brokers.

BK's Takeaways for Investors

Market Timing and Patience Matter

The deal spanned multiple market cycles (2006-2012). The initial deal failed during the market downturn and a $9.2M deposit was lost. Cal's patience to "sit on the asset until the market improved" paid off. Value fluctuated significantly ($368/SF in 2007 to $287/SF in 2011). A long-term perspective can overcome short-term market volatility.

Understand Zoning and Property Rights

Different zoning regulations created both challenges and opportunities. Mixed residential/commercial zoning affected property values differently, while subdividing along zoning boundaries maximized value. Air-rights and buildable square footage significantly influenced pricing. Understanding technical aspects can unlock hidden value.

Creative Deal Structures Create Value

Tax lot subdivision unlocked separate values for different uses and the joint venture structure kept reluctant sellers willing and motivated. The retail condo component satisfied one owner's concerns. Tax-efficient structuring enhanced returns. Flexibility in deal structure helped overcome obstacles. Understanding every stakeholder's objectives is key to getting deals done.

Rod's Lessons for Brokers:

Maintain Long-Term Client Relationships

Bob had prior deals with all major parties-multiple transactions, with the same clients over years. He returned to the same parties multiple times despite initial rejections. His trusted advisor status led to repeat business and long-term relationships enabled complex negotiations.

Create Solutions to Complex Problems

Bob identified an innovative subdivision strategy along zoning boundary. He found ways to satisfy multiple parties' needs and understood both technical (zoning) and personal (owner preferences) issues. When he proposed creative structures (retail condo, JV options), he added value through problem-solving rather than just transaction execution.

Persistence Through Market Cycles

Bob continued working on deals through the market downturn. He maintained relationships even when parties weren't ready to sell, trying multiple attempts and approaches over several years. He successfully navigated changing market conditions and adapted strategies as market conditions changed to complete complex assemblage.

This client success story demonstrates how complex deals require understanding of technical aspects (zoning, property rights), market dynamics, and human factors (relationships, timing, flexibility). Success came from combining all these elements over a multi-year period, showing the importance of both expertise and persistence in commercial real estate.

Rod's Reflections:

This is just one of the thousands of transactions BK has consummated over his career. Look at how many parties were involved. Including all the interested investors, it was well over twenty. Then, consider the complexity of the deal. There were multiple zoning factors and New York City's exclusive "air-rights." Finally, consider the real estate strategy. The continuing juggling of parties, personalities, contracts, and ultimately, the positioning of this land assemblage to create a win for all the owners.

This is certainly a unique situation. Most commercial real estate transactions focus on one property, one owner, or one space within a property. Most brokers can handle these straightforward transactions. However, commercial real estate authorities, like Bob Knakal, can orchestrate the complex and the unique and add significantly more value to the straightforward sale.

The Virgin Hotel deal lasted longer than the GFC. The GFC was a deep, long downturn, but the market came back, and so did the firms that survived.

The Market Hits Bottom and Recovery Begins

The market value bottomed out in the second half of 2010, and then, by 2011, things started to get really good, really fast. They say that these bad times are like stretching a rubber band down, and the lower you go, the more it bounces back. And that's exactly what happened here. I remember the 2010 activity was really terrible, value bottomed out, but then it came back in 2011 and was on fire. As soon as the market started to come back, we started hiring people back right away. So, we got back up to our 250-teammate headcount.

Coaching Magic

In 2011, I received a call from Rod, who said he was writing a book called *Brokers Who Dominate,* profiling brokers across North America who had achieved great success in commercial brokerage. "Several people have told me I have to profile you in my book. Would you have any interest in being profiled?" he asked. Of course, I said, "Okay." What broker wouldn't want to be profiled in a book with that title?

We set up a series of phone interviews, and Rod asked me about my practice and how I did the things I did. After a few sessions, I got around to asking Rod about his writing career. I asked him how many books he had written and was surprised to hear that this was his first book. I was further surprised to hear that his primary occupation was as a broker coach. Broker coach!! I didn't even know that existed.

Rod explained exactly what he did. He worked with brokers, dissecting their businesses, sharing best practices with them, and helping them grow their businesses. After listening to Rod explain what a broker coach does, it occurred to me that Tiger Woods had a coach, Michael Jordan had a coach, and Olympic athletes have coaches—why not give it a try?

Initially, I told Rod that I was happy with the money I was making; I just wanted to make the same amount of money and spend more time with my wife and daughter. Working with Rod was utterly eye-opening. Reviewing the fundamentals and thinking about each and every aspect of the business rekindled my passion for this business.

Working weekly with Rod not only rekindled my passion but made me much more effective and efficient. After just a few years of working together, my income had tripled from the best year I ever had AND I was spending more time with my family. It has been a life-changing experience for me, and Rod remains my coach to this day. If you are a broker and are not working with a coach, you are leaving hundreds of thousands, if not millions, of dollars on the table each year. Why forego that easy money when the answer is so simple?

Rod's Reflections:

I just started my coaching business, the Massimo Group, and was looking for people to coach. Every day, I seemed to hear about another person who had quit the business altogether or moved from a swanky downtown office to a desk in his bedroom. Folks were battening down the hatches. And I was looking for people to invest in themselves and our coaching.

In down times, people say, "The market is slow," in 2008 and 2009, people said, "The market is dead." And the market was dead. The only thing worse than a down market is an unknown market.

The Great Financial Crisis was the most severe economic downturn in my lifetime and it taught me, Bob, and other survivors lessons as well.

Since I was starting a new business, I was invisible to the marketplace. This required a total commitment to simply survive. And, for me, that meant sixteen-hour days. I would wake up at dawn, work all day, eat dinner with my wife and kids, and go back to work until 10 or 11—every day for over two years. Can you imagine how much further your business would be if you committed two years to total focus?

No matter how hard you work, you can't make the crisis go away. If you're going to survive a serious downturn, you need to figure out what's necessary. Your goal is to survive the downturn and be ready to accelerate when the market comes back.

Some of the things you must do won't be comfortable. In some cases, you are cutting costs; in others, you are investing more. I was taught to double down on your prospecting. It won't be easy, but it's essential. And if you are doubled down on prospecting, then go 4X on your marketing.

And get help. Transformation does not happen in isolation. Whether training or coaching, downtimes can be the best time to develop your skills and dominate when things improve.

As Bob shared above in 2011, we connected and started what is now a 13 year and running relationship.

But let me be completely transparent. When I first met BK, he was grossing $6 million a year in gross commissions. When he asked me to come to New York and visit and see if I could be of help, I asked myself, "What the hell can I do for this guy!" I quickly learned that everyone has room for exponential growth, even the very best.

Tax Policy Changes Affect the Market

2012 was awesome because a 3.8% capital gains tax was buried in Obamacare, and it was very covert. Nobody was talking about it. We knew about it. We wrote about it all over the place. I put it in every article. We put it in messages to our clients about tax policy.

It's very interesting. Warren Buffett has said numerous times that tax policy doesn't impact investor behavior. And I think when it comes to commercial real estate, that couldn't be further from the truth. I have nothing against Buffett and obviously, his investing success is unparalleled, but the fact is real estate markets are different from the stock markets. If you look at New York over the last 40 years, four out of the past five-sales volume peaks were created by tax policy changes.

Every percent that capital gains taxes go down is like a 1 percent increase in value. So, when you have these drops in capital gains taxes, the value goes up immediately. Whenever there's a tax reduction, it's usually retroactive to the beginning of the year. When they're going to increase capital gains taxes, it's almost never retroactive. It's usually prospective.

The Affordable Care Act, which everyone called "Obamacare," passed Congress in 2010. The main part of the law took effect on January 1, 2014, but the law included a Net Investment Income Tax that increased capital gains taxes by 3.8 percent. That part of the law took effect on January 1, 2013.

A lot of people wanted to sell to beat the tax increase. As a result, in 2012, 1,197 buildings sold in Manhattan, which is a record that still stands. 2014 was the biggest sales volume year for the city, when 5,534 buildings were sold. But, for Manhattan, the record was in 2012 as folks rushed to beat that capital gains tax increase.

We made a third of our annual total for 2012 in the fourth quarter. On New Year's Eve of 2012, I think we closed 33 or 34 deals. Tax policy clearly impacts market participant behavior in commercial real estate investment sales.

Rod's Wrap-Up

The beautiful thing about Bob and many of our coaching clients is that they aren't focused on "How much was this going to cost me?" Instead, Bob asked himself, "How much can coaching help me?" As it turns out, the answer was" exponentially". Bob would go on to triple his already impressive gross revenue within three years of our meeting,

I've experienced at least six major "downturns." It has become painfully obvious that when things get bad, people fall into three categories---Panic, Petrified, or Proactive. The panicked ones leave the industry, never to return. The petrified ones become indecisive and do nothing. The proactive ones become the next market leaders.

When the times start to get good again, the proactive are ready to move quickly. You heard how Bob and Paul started hiring people back as soon as they could. Likewise, by 2012, the Massimo Group became the best-known commercial real estate brokerage coaching organization in the US. Today, we are the leading CRE brokerage coaching firm in the world.

2012 was a great comeback year for Massey Knakal commercial real estate in New York City. It was also the year that Massey Knakal faced another major inflection point and had to make another decision about how to scale the business. That's what you'll read in the next chapter.

SELLING FOR MAXIMUM PRICE – $100 MILLION OFFERS

The Great Financial Crisis was the hardest of times for Bob and Paul in terms of running Massey Knakal. The Savings & Loan Crisis in the early 1990s almost bankrupted the company, but the partners didn't have to lay off dozens of teammates, so the emotional toll during the GFC was much more difficult for them to deal with. But when the market rebounded after the GFC, it came roaring back.

Massey Knakal was about to have its best years ever. Beginning in late 2010, people were hired back, all the New York City territories were filled again, and by mid-2011, market activity was rolling along at a great clip. Bob and Paul faced a major choice about what to do next. Their decision led to another major inflection point for the company.

In this chapter, you'll learn why they chose to do this, why they decided to sell Massey Knakal, and how they sold their business using the same techniques they used to sell so many buildings at the highest possible price.

All the New York City Territories are Full

By late 2010, it was clear the market was bottoming out and the "green shoots" everyone talks about when describing the start of a recovery were evident. We decided to have our human resource folks get back into full swing and hire folks to fill the positions we had to eliminate to make it through the Great Financial Crisis.

By mid-2011, we were back at full strength, with producers occupying all New York City territories. Values started to pop back up, and optimism abounded. The national healthcare law was being negotiated and contained a covert capital gains tax, which would increase that tax in 2013. Market participants have historically reacted sharply to tax law changes, and 2012 was no different. 2012 was an awesome year, with 1198 buildings sold in the Manhattan submarket – the highest total ever for the submarket. 2013 was great. 2014 was beyond the best with 5,534 buildings sold citywide – an all-time record by more than 10% which still stands to this day.

Our office was at capacity in 2011, and we faced another big decision. We faced a similar decision in 1999 when all of the territories in Manhattan were filled, and we had to choose between geographic expansion or service line increases. Then, we chose geographic expansion and opened offices in Queens and Brooklyn. If we were to do the same thing again, we would have to go farther afield.

This time, we considered going to Chicago, Boston, Philly, DC, or getting into other service lines like debt, retail leasing, or office leasing. Our Advisory Board probably saved us early in the Great Financial Crisis by suggesting that cutting overhead quickly was necessary. In 2011, their shared wisdom helped us navigate this next inflection point. Their input was instrumental in this important decision.

What Shall We Do?

Should we expand geographically or add service lines? The circumstances we looked at in 2011 were very different from those we faced in 1999. If we were going to go to Chicago, which would have been our next market, we would have to explain to folks who we were and then what we did. In New York City, we had decades of relationships with local owners who knew us, liked us, and wanted to work with us. We decided to add services and leverage the brand awareness we built over the prior 23 years in New York City.

We quickly realized that office leasing was a very different business than what we were doing and that mortgage brokerage and retail leasing were much more synergistic than other service lines. Appraisal didn't have great margins, and property management was full of headaches, so we ruled them out fairly quickly.

We got into retail leasing. Paul and I had two different motivations for getting into this business. Paul wanted to make it a profitable division. I was interested in the business mostly for the advertising benefits the company would get from all the storefront signage the business would provide. We never made profits in the retail leasing business, but I liked it anyway. The signage was tremendous advertising that didn't cost us anything as the business broke even for us. Having another 70 or 80 signs on the ground level of buildings to join the hundreds of For Sale signs around town gave us tremendous brand exposure.

John Fowler, a member of our Advisory Board, was a great mortgage broker and one of the named partners in Holliday Fegnolio & Fowler (HFF). He convinced us to get into the debt business, suggesting we could make a lot of money by stapling financing onto our property sales. The debt business turned out to be great for us.

We started gearing up for it in 2011 and hired a couple of people. 2012 was the first full year we were really in that space and we did about $300 million in debt in that first year. In 2013, we did $800 million, and in 2014, we did $1.3 billion in debt. Both those service lines were accretive to our business.

Rod's Reflections:

There is no one "best" strategy that will work every time for every business. When Massey Knakal filled the Manhattan territories, expanding geographically into the outer boroughs made sense because it allowed them to build on their strengths. The boroughs were full of the kind of properties that Massey Knakal specialized in. There was very little organized competition at that time. And Massey Knakal's marketing system would set their new brokers up to succeed.

There were three major inflection points for Massey Knakal. The first was in 1999 when all the Manhattan sales territories were filled, and Bob and Paul needed to decide to expand to other service lines or, geographically, to other boroughs. Expanding outside New York City would be much harder than expanding into the boroughs had been. The second was deciding what to do after 9/11, when everyone was downsizing. Bob and Paul had an unwavering belief in the future of NYC and counterintuitively went on a hiring spree. In this third key inflection point, the situation was very different. By 2014, Massey Knakal was coming off its three best sales years, as the services they began providing in 2011 had grown and added nicely to the company's revenue. It was time to revisit a decision Bob and Paul made in 2007. To sell or not to sell?

Deciding to Sell Massey Knakal

Back in 2007, after it was apparent that the CBRE deal was not going to happen, we learned a valuable lesson. That lesson was that a brokerage business is a service business, and a service business generally doesn't have any patents, doesn't manufacture any products, and doesn't really have much to sell other than its people. During the negotiations with CBRE, we learned that any buyer would want Paul and me to be on 5-year service contracts post-sale.

So, we decided that 2014 would be a good time to investigate selling because Paul would turn 55 in February of 2015, and the perception of the value of those contracts would be much higher if we were in our fifties instead of in our eighties. So, in 2007, we decided to explore a sale in 2014 if the market wasn't in bad shape. As fate would have it, and completely unbeknownst to us in 2007 when we made that decision, 2014 would become the perfect time to sell.

How to Get the Best Price

How were we going to sell the firm? In our business, we always tell a seller to hire us exclusively, have us put together a comprehensive marketing package, maximize the asset's exposure to the market, create a competitive bidding process, and professionally handle the entire program.

We knew the owners of every brokerage company operating in New York City. We could just go to them ourselves. But just as we advise our clients not to "do it themselves," we decided to take our own advice and hire professionals. We interviewed a few firms and decided to retain Perella Weinberg. We met with reps from the firm and had a very good feeling about them, given other service businesses they had sold and their understanding of our business. We hired Perella, and they helped us significantly.

At the beginning of the process, we were unsure what reception we would get. We didn't have to sell, but we wanted to sell. But how could we convey that sentiment to the potential buyers? We said, alright, when we sell buildings, even if the seller has to sell, we want to create the appearance the seller doesn't have to sell and that the seller has other options. We needed to create the same appearance for us.

So, we had Perella launch the sales process for the company and, at the same time, decided to continue with business as usual and, in fact, initiated some new campaigns. We went out and spent probably $100 to $150 grand on a rebranding campaign. We were going to change the logo slightly and change the color scheme slightly in an attempt to modernize the brand. In our meetings with potential buyers, we said, "Yeah, we're undergoing a rebranding strategy to freshen up the company."

We operated up until the day of the closing as if we were going to keep operating the business for another 20 years because we couldn't get into a place where we would become so committed to the sale that it would be obvious we had passed the point of no return and couldn't back out. Like selling a building, the leverage of having options, whether real or perceived, is invaluable.

Rod's Reflections:

Bob and Paul created a system for selling buildings for the best possible price. You heard about their five-phase marketing program in the chapter on "Building Out the Company." They used those same techniques to get the best possible price for their company.

Those principles are basic sales principles. Use them to sell buildings, companies, or anything else.

Bob and Paul knew they needed outside help. This would be the biggest transaction of their personal and professional lives, so they hired an investment banker with the experience to get them the maximum value for their business—the same reason so many New York City owners hire Bob to sell their buildings.

How Much is a Service Business Worth?

Massey Knakal's sale process played out much differently than we had anticipated. We probably had 10 or 12 offers, and it was the weirdest thing – so different from a building sale. When you sell a building, you have the meaty part of your bell curve of offers that is 10% or 15% below the final sale price, and there are a few lower offers and a few that are at the higher end. Our distribution of bids for the company was so crazy. I think our low bid was just $26 million, and we had bids of $39, $47, $55, $61, $68, $72, $89 – and then two at $100 million.

The bids were all over the place. I'm an investment sales guy, and I'm not used to that. In my experience, bids are usually tightly clustered, and seeing this tremendously wide range was shocking.

I think that's indicative of the fact that nobody knows what a service business is really worth. It's worth what somebody's willing to pay for it, and what somebody's willing to pay has a lot to do with the impact the acquisition will have on the buyer's company and how the acquired company will be incorporated into the buyer's business.

Two 100 Million Dollar Bids

I think the reason we were getting a premium from both Cushman & Wakefield (C&W) and Meridian, the two $100 million bids, was the impact that we would have on the buyer's underlying business. C&W expressed significant interest immediately. At the time, the company was being run by Ed Forst, an investment banker brought in by the Agnelli family, who owned C&W. Unbeknownst to us at the time, Ed was brought in to position the company for a sale of the entire business. C&W had a doughnut hole in capital markets in New York City, and filling that hole was necessary for the perception buyers would have when they looked at buying C&W. If we were more perceptive, we could have figured out that Forst's hiring was a foreshadow of a potential company sale, but we weren't.

When Meridian expressed interest, we didn't know what to expect. They were the leading mortgage brokerage business in New York City at the time, and the synergies seemed obvious to us. Ralph Hertzka is a titan of the finance world, and their interest seemed genuine. I think Meridian realized that being able to staple financing onto a significant percentage of a robust sales platform would be tremendously accretive to them. They looked at our revenue not as whatever we had—$92 or $93 million of revenue—but as $150 million of revenue because of the marginal increase in revenue they would get from being able to staple financing on a lot of our deals.

And then I think some of the low bids probably just looked at it as a standalone business and hey, this is a peak time, and it's not going to always be a peak time. The lower bids looked at it as just a standalone, and the high bids looked at how it would impact the company moving forward.

Ed Forst came out of the gate fast and hard. Ed's first offer was great at $100 million – "I figured you guys weren't a seller below that price," he told us. But the terms were not great. Cushman's first bid was 25% cash and 75% on a 5-year earnout, which would've been a total disaster based on what happened in the market in subsequent years.

To our surprise, after a couple of all-hands-on-deck meetings, Meridian came in very competitively. They offered $100 million on much better terms than Cushman was offering.

We decided to call Ed and tell him, "If we had to decide today, we would not sell the business to you guys." Knowing what we know now, Ed must have freaked out. Leverage, baby, it means everything.

At this time, Paul and I owned 84% of the company, with nine other partners owning the other 16%. We discussed all the bids with the partners and generally reached a good consensus.

Two days later, C&W completely changed their terms. They went from 25% cash with a 5-year earnout to 75% cash and the other 25% in three years if we stayed with the company and nine years later if we left after the sale closed. No earnout at all. How great was that? Ed had to have us, and the terms were acceptable. If the Meridian offer wasn't there, it would've been a much worse deal. So, by leveraging the Meridian offer, we were able to get Cushman to come back with 75% cash and 25% cash three years later.

That's why we try to get multiple people to the table for our clients when we are selling a building, and it's a big reason why an exclusive listing is the best way to sell a property. If you're just dealing with open-listed brokers, they represent one buyer, and they want to make that deal. You're negotiating with one buyer, and you have much less leverage than if you're negotiating with other people and you have multiple bids. We drank our own Kool-Aid.

It's a fundamental part of selling anything. And so, I think it's so interesting how we saw in our practice that if you have multiple competitive bids and you send out multiple contracts, you get such a better result. That couldn't have been more illustrative than what happened in selling the business.

CLIENT SUCCESS STORY: THERE ARE ALMOST ALWAYS OBSTACLES

Thor Equities had owned a functioning multi-story parking facility with ground floor retail at 300 Livingston Street, located at the intersection of Bond and Livingston Streets in Downtown Brooklyn since 2007. By late 2012, they wanted to sell. With the growth of the Brooklyn market, the potential 600,000-square-foot development site would be an attractive investment for many investors and developers.

However, there were several issues that were problematic. First, the site was encumbered by a tenant with a 60-plus-year lease for the loading docks. Second, the basement and underground passageway (right of way) leading across Livingston Street made the future development of the site very challenging. Third, an adjacent subway line and MTA easement made construction on the southern portion of the site very difficult and potentially cost-prohibitive.

These factors, in conjunction with height restrictions and setback requirements, seemed to prevent the total allowable buildable square footage from being massed and ultimately reduced the potential maximum value of the site.

Understanding they needed an advisor who could address all these issues, Thor hired us exclusively to market the site because of all of the development sites we had sold, many of which had complications. The Downtown Brooklyn submarket was on fire, but the obstacles had to be overcome.

Recognizing the construction difficulties at the site, we did several things to overcome the hurdles and get a great result for the seller. We focused the bulk of our efforts on those parties that we knew had the expertise to deal with the site's rather unusual encumbrances. We consulted with attorneys, architects, and engineers to better understand the site and contacted the long-term tenant to begin buyout discussions, as that tenant had to be vacated in order to maximize the development value. We also arranged meetings with adjacent owners to see if the site could be enlarged in order to shift the bulk of the development away from the problem areas and allow the site to be fully massed.

After working with several groups, TF Cornerstone exhibited the experience to deal with each of these obstacles and had, in fact, dealt with and overcame each one before! We sold them the site for $70,000,000, or $140 per as-of-right buildable square foot, which, even with the site's challenges, was in excess of the original reconciled value we delivered to Thor.

Here are three key takeaways from this deal story for commercial real estate investors and brokers.

BK's Takeaways for Investors

Due Diligence on Complex Issues

Multiple complicated issues affected the property, including a 60+ year lease for loading docks, basement, and underground passageway rights, subway line and MTA easement, and height restrictions and setback requirements. Successful investors needed expertise in handling complex sites. Understanding all constraints before purchase is crucial. Previous experience with similar issues adds value. TF Cornerstone succeeded because they had dealt with each obstacle before.

Value Creation Through Problem-Solving

Site challenges created opportunities for experienced developers who understood how to overcome physical constraints. Their ability to negotiate with long-term tenants, knowledge of working with adjacent owners, and technical expertise in construction near transit infrastructure, positioned the developer to differentiate themselves and win the deal.

Look Beyond Surface Limitations

600,000 square foot development potential existed despite constraints. Market conditions (Downtown Brooklyn "on fire") supported development. Creative solutions can unlock value. Working with adjacent owners could create additional opportunities. Technical solutions could overcome physical constraints. You have to be creative and set yourself apart as the buyer of choice. It is not always just about the price.

Rod's Lessons for Brokers

Match Properties with the Right Buyers

Focused marketing on buyers with relevant expertise.
Targeted those with experience handling similar issues.
Understanding buyer capabilities is crucial.
Identified buyers who could see past problems to opportunity.
Found buyer (TF Cornerstone) with specific relevant experience.

Build Expert Networks

Bob consulted with attorneys for legal issues, worked with architects on development potential, and engaged engineers for technical solutions. He initiated discussions with the long-term tenant and coordinated with adjacent property owners.

Comprehensive Problem Analysis

Bob identified all major obstacles upfront and developed strategies for each challenge. He understood how different issues interacted. He created solutions before marketing and presented solutions alongside problems. Proactively addressing these issues prior to marketing saves precious time and effort on the backend.

This client success story demonstrates how complex properties require a sophisticated approach from both investors and brokers. Success came from understanding all challenges, developing specific solutions, and matching the property with buyers who had the right expertise. The final price ($70M, $140/BSF) exceeded original valuations despite the challenges, showing how proper handling of obstacles can lead to superior results.

Rod's Wrap-Up

When Bob and Paul decided it was time to sell, Massey Knakal found motivated buyers at the peak of the market. It's easy to look at that and think it was just good luck. But luck is the residue of design and smart, purposeful work.

Bob and Paul created a company that other companies would want to buy. They hired well, seized opportunities, and developed a system that made it more likely they would achieve the best price for any property they sold. They also created a system in which scaling was possible without cannibalization or having teammates trip over each other. They acted to increase their presence in the market. They forged relationships with clients and with people in the industry. They positioned the business to be top of mind through constant market presence and proof-stacking. And the company was remarkably dominant in its space, lapping the field by more than three times in at least the last 14 of its 26 years.

They also turbocharged their opportunity. They sought outside help from an advisory board and engaged an investment bank to handle their company sale process. They used what they learned selling buildings for the best possible price to sell their company for the best possible price.

If this were a fairy tale, the story would end here. Bob and Paul would ride off into the sunset with saddlebags stuffed with cash. The sale certainly worked out well for Bob and Paul financially, but there are many other important things in life. That's why the next chapter is called "That Pot of Gold Doesn't Come With a Rainbow."

THAT POT OF GOLD DOESN'T COME WITH A RAINBOW

$100 million is a lot of money! It certainly counts as a big score, and many people believe that if you make a big score, everything will be great from that point on. But the truth is that a singular success, no matter how great it is, does not mean permanent success.

Living happily ever after is a myth. Whether you make a great deal, win the lottery, marry the person of your dreams, or sell your company for $100 million, life goes on, filled with ups and downs and new challenges.

For Bob, the weeks after the sale of Massey Knakal were full of introspection. Yes, there was the five-year contract with Cushman & Wakefield, but he was trying to figure out how this life-changing amount of money would change his life.

Would he start to slow down? After all, the payouts from the buyout would flow whether he worked or not. 75% of the cash was upfront, and the other 25% would be paid in three years if you stayed at the firm or in nine years if you left the firm at any point after closing but before the three-year anniversary.

Would he start to invest in properties and shy away from brokerage? Would he just go to live on Grand Cayman and spend his days lounging on Seven Mile Beach, one of his favorite places on Earth?

Ultimately, Bob decided that being a broker is what he truly loves. He has often said that being an investment sales broker is his career and his hobby. His competitive nature is satiated by the variety of "wins" the business provides. There's a win when you find out the client wants to sell, the win when you get awarded the exclusive after the pitch, the win when you get a meeting of the minds between a buyer and the seller, the win when the contract is signed, and the win when the transaction closes. Bob became addicted to winning and wasn't about to stop or even slow down.

As his coach since 2011, I have seen his insatiable desire to win drive him and make him one of the best, if not the best, commercial brokers in the world. He has a burning desire to work hard, understand the business better than anyone else, and achieve the best possible results for his clients.

Bob was going to stay committed to brokering, but he also used to be the owner. At Cushman & Wakefield, he went from being the co-founder and Chairman of the most successful investment sales firm by a wide margin in the most competitive market on the planet to working for someone else. That was a major truth about Bob's new reality. Much of that reality would not be pretty.

Bob went from a boutique firm to a globe-spanning giant that would become publicly traded. The transition was more difficult than he ever imagined. But not for the reasons you might guess.

In this chapter, we will examine the differences between small and big firms, boutique firms, and globe-spanning firms. First though, we'll look at the timing and causes of the market correction that was right around the corner.

Market Cycles

We sold Massey Knakal on December 31, 2014. The market was still at a fever pitch. More buildings were sold in New York City that year than ever before or since by a margin of more than 10%. Yes, it was indeed the perfect time to sell but, as you have read, the decision about timing was made years earlier.

2015 started out exceptionally well. The sales volume was $80.1 billion, a record for New York City. Those were just unbelievably great years and probably the most fun years in my career up to that point. And those good times started back in 2011, so we had five great years of increasing volumes and values. It was as close to nirvana as a market could get.

When you have an unbelievably great run like this, it never stays. It is a temporary thing. As I always say, the market has always been, is, and always will be cyclical, and this period was no different. So, we had this incredible run, but the run was clearly coming to an end, and the market started to go the other way.

Why does this happen? What drives the cycle? When times are good, folks start to deploy capital. As they deploy capital, those bets look increasingly smart. And the bets pay off. So, more bets are made. Land is purchased for construction. New buildings are being built. Eventually, the new supply exerts downward pressure on rents, and then values fall, and the correction begins. This cycle was just like this.

During the first two weeks of October 2015, it was clear the bull market was over. We were getting strong signals from both the land and hotel markets that the music was ending. Those two sectors are most predictive of changes in the market because they are the most sensitive to market shifts. Hotels have leases for just one day, and land is a proxy for what developers believe market conditions will be like in 3 to 5 years when what they are building will come to market to be rented or sold. Within two or three weeks, we saw hotel cap rates go up by 75 to 100 basis points, and the offers we were getting on development sites were 15% to 20% below what we had anticipated.

I remember very well that the Cayre family hired us in June of 2015 to sell a development site in Brooklyn at 205 Montague Street. This was a big site and was going to change the nature of that market. It had 350,000 buildable feet right in downtown Brooklyn, a great location.

They wanted a super-duper, high-end marketing package that we worked on for almost three months. We were ready to launch in mid-October, but we had to go into their offices and tell them we missed the market. We had about 40 development sites on the market that summer, and by the end of September / early October, all of the bids were coming in way below what we had anticipated. This is one of the advantages of specialization and having a large market share. Had we had only a handful of sites on the market, we may not have seen the trend in such a pronounced manner. But it was clear as day.

I'll tell you what it's like. Imagine you're on a frozen lake, walking across the lake, and you start to hear that crackling. What's that sound? That was October 1st through October 15th. You hear the crackling all around you. You haven't seen the cracks in the ice yet, but you hear them. And others are obliviously walking across the ice with headphones on without a care in the world – but you know how it will end. As of the writing of this book in 2024, 205 Montague still has not been sold. By mid-2016, you started to see the cracks. Then you knew what was going to happen. You knew you were going through the ice.

2016 was the quintessential change-of-direction year in the market, with a deviation between real value and comparable sale value. This differentiation is not in any appraisal handbook, but the dynamic certainly exists. Most of the market understood that values had changed. But some investors were ignorantly still bidding yesterday's price. And what happens is that comp sale value seems to go up as sellers who get yesterday's price pull the trigger and sell. Those that don't, take their properties off the market and don't transact. We advised many clients not to buy in 2016, and those that didn't thanked us. If you look at the statistics, values did go up in 2016 by about 6%, but volume dropped like a stone. You always see this in the transitional year when the good market ends.

From October 2015 through February 2020, the dollar volume of sales dropped by 56%. The number of properties sold dropped by 54%, and values were down about 10 to 12% if you aggregated all property types.

The main reason the market started to crack in October of 2015 was that there was a realization that the condo market was not a bottomless pit of buyers who would pay continually increasing prices. And a ton of residential rental supply was brought to the market based on all those land sales from 2011 through 2014. So, downward pressure was exerted on residential rents. If the condo market was squishy and rents began to get soft, what would conditions be like in 3-5 years? This impacted the psyche of developers, and land sales activity slowed. If rents were not going to rise, what did that do to the financial models being run by folks looking to purchase existing assets? Things were getting challenging, and it was much tougher to get deals done.

Rod's Reflections:

Whether you're a broker or an investor, this is a movie you'll watch many times in your career. The market heats up, doing business is easy, and everybody's happy. The details are different every time, but the truth remains the same. What goes up must come down. When it does, everything gets harder.

In Bob's case, things also got harder on a personal level. It was hard to fit his entrepreneurial spirit into a corporate environment and adjust to his new role. To make things more challenging, Cushman & Wakefield made moves as they prepared to go public, and Bob's relationship with Paul was changing.

Bob's New World

The early part of the Cushman transition was very, very easy. We stayed in the same office space at 275 Madison where we had three floors and about 45,000 square feet. They basically sent over new business cards and let Paul and me run the show. Everything else was the same. We just had different branding on all of our materials. The guy who was responsible for running New York for Cushman would come over to our office once a month and just walk around for a while and say hi to everyone. And then he was out of there. We were really very, very self-sufficient, and all of our folks were very happy.

I was the top capital markets producer globally at Cushman for four years, from 2014 to 2017. It was mainly because they left us alone and let what worked work.

Then, in the fall of 2016, Cushman made a move to bring Doug Harmon, Adam Spies and their team over from Eastdil. At the time, they were the top team in the United States in terms of the large institutional sales space. I don't blame the company for doing this. If I ran the company, I would have done it also if I had the opportunity. But that move was a breach of all our contracts. Adam and Doug were given the keys to the castle and didn't want to share them. We shortened our contracts from five years to three and a half years, got a few more bucks and some additional support, and tried to make the best of it.

Then in mid-17, they relocated our offices to Cushman's main office at 1290 Sixth Avenue and tried to integrate us. But the Eastdil guys were in their own segregated wing of the office. The efforts to combine the operations failed miserably.

We had the investment sales platform that had the most building sales by number of properties sold and the investment sales platform that had the highest dollar volume of sales under one roof. But management couldn't figure out how to make that work. It was the single greatest opportunity I have seen in the brokerage business in New York City in the past 40 years, and it completely evaporated.

Cushman & Wakefield's IPO

By late 2017, Cushman & Wakefield was preparing to make an initial public offering. That influenced all their decisions and sucked up a lot of time. The IPO wasn't going to be easy. They had more than $3 billion in debt, far more than their competition. They lost money in 2016, 2017, and the first quarter of 2018.

All of our key Massey Knakal folks had contracts expiring on June 30th, 2018. By early 2018, it was clear I did not want to stay at C&W, so I started speaking to other firms. That was a mistake.

Even in a big market like New York City, the world is small, and even a quiet conversation in an obscure location would somehow get back to the C & W management. After the first time it happened, I let them know I was unhappy there and was going to be speaking to other firms. They tried to work something out, but we just weren't going to be able to co-exist with Harmon and Spies. It was time for me to move on, and many of our key folks also wanted out. I wasn't the only one; many were disillusioned by the way things were going given how our old platform was being marginalized.

Paul's situation had also changed significantly. In late 2016, he took a leave of absence from Cushman to run for mayor of New York City. During 2017, he campaigned daily and was completely out of the brokerage business. After his campaign ended, he did not return to the business immediately. After thirty years of building a business together, we headed in different directions.

After C&W, Then What?

I wanted to go to another company and not start my own thing again at the end of our C&W contract because I thought, "Hey, the market could crash again." The market wasn't great to begin with, and who knew what it would be like moving forward? And it was so emotional for me to have to fire 25% of our staff in 2008, and that feeling was still far too fresh a memory to me, even ten years later. I didn't want to go there again.

Many of the senior producers who were with me at C&W were also with me at Massey Knakal and wanted to leave also. Many of us wanted to stay together. So, we thought, let's go to one of these big firms, and if the ice breaks, we'll be safe there.

In June 2018, Cushman made one last, unusual attempt to keep me. Sometime during the last week in June, they called me at 10 am and offered me $5 million to stay for three years. The catch was I had to accept by 5 pm that day! I asked if I could talk it over with my wife and was told I could speak to anyone I wanted as long as I got back to them by 5 pm. I didn't respond and by 5:15, my phone was blowing up. A friend told me there was an article in The Real Deal saying Cushman had fired me. That's how I found out.

I spent that summer negotiating employment contracts with JLL, Meridian, and another firm. At the end of the process, the group voted to go to JLL. So, I went there with 53 of my friends. I have been told that this was the largest mass exodus from a commercial brokerage firm in the US without a company being purchased.

Rod's Reflections:

Clearly, Bob doesn't think much of working for a big corporate firm if you are focusing on investment sales. That's OK. That's what's right for him. However, Bob's perspective is not right for every broker. And to his credit, Bob always talks about the pros and cons that exist at all firms, regardless of size or type. He always says, "take advantage of the pros and try to avoid the cons."

At the Massimo Group, we have clients all over the world who deliver significant value to their clients. Some of them are like Bob, but many are not. There are excellent brokers working for giants like Cushman & Wakefield, CBRE, or JLL, excellent brokers working for boutique firms, and excellent brokers who started their own firms.

If you're a broker, your challenge is to figure out where you work best. Where you can do your best work and deliver the most value to your client? That's the name of the game in brokerage. If you're an investor, what matters to you is the effectiveness of your broker. As we've seen elsewhere in the book, many investors follow brokers from firm to firm because those brokers deliver value.

There is a massive difference between leasing, debt, and investment sales. For example, in the leasing world, you must provide a ton of services. You don't just go to a client who needs 200,000 square feet and do the deal yourself. You need project development services, workplace environment expertise, and all these other things for which you need a big team. The big shops magnify and clarify these significant differences between the different types of brokerage businesses.

If you are a broker, you must figure out where you will deliver the most value to your clients. If you're an investor, you must decide which broker will give you the best value, regardless of their platform. Bob's experience illustrates the importance of delivering value.

CLIENT SUCCESS STORY: HEY BABY, HOW ABOUT A BUYOUT

When it comes to land assemblage, there is nothing that can compare to New York City. Because there are not rolling fields of open land in New York City, land "assemblage" is the way to create a site upon which to build new buildings. Assemblage is the practice of acquiring many smaller assets owned by several different owners in order to create a buildable development site.

To create the ability to do the sale of this 75,000 buildable square foot site, the seller worked tirelessly over several years to purchase each of the component assets. There was one "holdout" owner (the term used for an owner that won't sell even if the price is well in excess of the market) in the middle of the block. To induce this holdout to sell, the owner publicly stated that they were going to build low-income housing projects on the balance of the land they acquired. Before you knew it, the holdout seller was happy to take a reasonable price.

That left the tenants, some of which were commercial and some of which were rent regulated residential tenants, as issues to deal with as well as complicated zoning issues. Rent regulated tenants have a right to renew their leases. You cannot just decide not to renew their leases when they expire. We were retained to sell the site prior to the tenants being vacated and began the marketing process telling buyers that the seller would vacate the premises and that we could work around the zoning issues.

A pizza shop with about one year to go was paid about $150,000 to leave early. A few of the residential rent regulated tenants were bought out at reasonable amounts, which left one tenant who was presumably a free-market tenant who should be able to be vacated at the expiration of their lease.

After a comprehensive marketing process, we signed a contract at an astounding price of $69,600,000 or $926 per buildable square foot – but it was contingent upon getting the last tenant out. This is where things get very complicated in New York City. Tenants can be rent controlled or rent stabilized and in either case, the tenants don't have to leave if they don't want to. Prior to 2019, you could take a previously rent controlled or rent stabilized unit and deregulate it in a number of ways.

That last tenant happened to be a prostitute (verified by the seller based upon Craig's List ads) who, although a non-regulated tenant, could have made a claim that they were rent regulated, as tenants can claim anything, and get over a year in New York City's Landlord / Tenant Court to stay in the apartment as the investigation commences. Given the massive price that we had obtained for the seller, we advised the seller to pay whatever was necessary to get the tenant out. After weeks of negotiating, the prostitute was paid $850,000 to leave.

Based upon the title of this piece, I had a reader email me to basically yell at me for being demeaning to women for using "Baby" with regard to the prostitute. As it turns out, the prostitute was, in fact, a man.

Here are three key takeaways from this deal story for commercial real estate investors and brokers.

BK's Takeaways for Investors

Understand Tenant Rights and Buyout Costs

Understanding tenant rights is critical for any investor, particularly in a complex market like New York City. Rent-regulated tenants enjoy substantial protections, and even non-regulated tenants can claim regulated status, dragging the process through lengthy legal challenges. Buyout costs can be staggering, as this one case illustrated with a payment of $850,000 to remove a single tenant. Investors must budget for these potential costs during acquisition planning and be prepared for delays. I recently sold a development site on Manhattan's Upper East Side where the developer paid $10 million to buy out two rent-stabilized tenants.

Strategic Assembly Tactics

Strategic assembly is another vital consideration. This process requires careful maneuvering, including leveraging public statements or negotiating tailored solutions for different types of tenants, whether commercial or residential. In some cases, paying a premium for buyouts is the only way to move a project forward successfully, as seen with the pizza shop and other tenants in this case.

Account for all Contingencies

Lastly, investors must anticipate and plan for contingencies. Tenant removal, zoning challenges, and unexpected legal hurdles can significantly impact deal timelines and costs. However, these issues must be balanced against the potential value of the asset, as the remarkable $69.6 million sale price in this example demonstrated. Sometimes, absorbing higher costs is justified by the broader success of the project.

Rod's Lessons for Brokers

Deal Structure and Contingencies

Structuring deals with contingencies is sometimes necessary. This includes understanding tenant laws, anticipating potential claims and delays, and crafting strategies to address tenant buyouts. Advising clients to weigh price against buyout costs can ensure transactions proceed smoothly and deliver the desired outcomes.

Market Value Assessment

Brokers must also excel at market value assessment. Recognizing true asset value, as seen in the $69.6 million deal, involves evaluating risks, advising on premium buyouts when necessary, and calculating price metrics like buildable square foot values. Knowing when additional costs are warranted can make or break a deal.

Advising Client on Strategic Solutions

Problem-solving is a core skill brokers need to master. Whether it's navigating tenant rights, managing client expectations, or recommending creative solutions like "pay whatever is necessary," brokers must focus on the ultimate goal: delivering value to their clients. It's not just about marketing a property; it's about guiding clients through the complexities of real estate transactions with expertise and foresight.

This client success story demonstrates the requirement of balancing high acquisition costs against buyout expenses while navigating complex legal and practical challenges. Bob's role went beyond traditional marketing to include strategic advisory on tenant removal and deal structuring.

Size Matters But Not Always the Same Way

I think the benefits of being at a large global firm really depend on what area of the business you are in. I think investors go with big firms seeking a kind of one-stop shop with all the broker specialties and services they'll need under one roof. However, this approach does not necessarily mean you will get the best professional in each discipline within the market.

Just because folks have the same business card doesn't mean they are all equal in their standing within the market. And "bulk discounts" rarely apply if you use multiple services at the same company. As an investor, I think you still want to make sure the broker you work with can deliver value for you. If you are selling a building, you only get one chance. There are no "do-overs" if you don't do it right the first time. That's more important than the range of services a firm can provide.

As it has always been, it's all about the client, producing great results for the client, and doing everything you can to help the client achieve their objectives. It's not about you.

Adding Value in Investment Sales

At Massey Knakal, we were so successful because we became experts to the point where we added tangible value to the client. That value and expertise allowed the client to receive execution they couldn't receive anywhere else. The true market expert knows the market better than anyone else and, therefore, has better insights into how things will play out. That insight leads to a higher probability of decision-making for clients, better execution, and better bottom-line results. The more expertise the broker has, the more informed the client is and the more informed the client is, the better decisions they can make.

Market expertise in investment sales means somebody who knows all the comps (inside and out), all the buyers and where they are getting their capital and their tendencies, who the sellers are and why they are selling, the zoning in the submarkets, the new tenants moving in who are changing the face of the landscape, and the new developments that are underway and in planning that will profoundly change the future of various locations within the local market. As a broker who only represented sellers and only on an exclusive basis, this expertise allowed us to be the best advocate possible to convince buyers why they should pay more for a particular property, bringing real, tangible value to our clients and their balance sheets.

Regarding the investment sales business in New York, we understood that in Manhattan the average annual turnover rate of the entire stock of buildings was 2.6% over the long term. In the outer boroughs, the turnover rate has been 2.2%. Based on this reality, we divided up the market into territories that were small enough for our brokers to be the true market experts while large enough for them to make a great living. Our approach was statistically based and empirical.

Expertise Matters

Based on this analysis, I think the perfect target list for an investment sales broker should be about 1,000 to 1200 property owners. That likely represents 5,000 to 10,000 properties. If we use Manhattan as a proxy for what happens around this country, that's about 260 sales annually. If you get a 20% market share (which was always the target), that's 52 deals you could do in a year. If you are doing 52 deals in a year, that's a great income for anyone. The 1,000 to 1,200 target owners is manageable if you make 80 to 100 connections weekly. At that rate, you can speak to each owner every quarter which is a great frequency considering the average owner in Manhattan owns a building for an average of 40 years after purchasing it. That is derived from the 2.6% turnover rate.

This was the main ingredient in how Massey Knakal became so dominant. We really became neighborhood experts. We knew every single owner, details of every transaction, and had a command of every market metric. We studied the sales and spoke to each buyer and seller. We knew what zoning changes were happening before they were implemented and what new developments were happening that could change the landscape.

In the sales world in Manhattan, from 2001 to 2014, we lapped the field by more than three times in terms of the number of properties we sold. The number 2 company sold about 1,300 properties while Massey Knakal sold over 4,000. Where have you ever seen that?

In the 1980s and 1990s, there were many more synergies within geography than within property type. Publicly available information was so opaque back then, and what was available was highly inaccurate. Getting to really know the neighborhood was a differentiator and created real value for our clients. Today, if we took that same approach, it would be much less effective, given the massive amount, and accuracy, of publicly available information.

If you Google someone today, you get all of their contact information, their cell number, their shoe size, and even their favorite flavor of ice cream. Everything is so transparent that geographically oriented market information is not a big deal. Today, being a property sector expert is much more important and an easier way to differentiate yourself. It also is a magnificent way to "create time" by making every minute working accretive towards getting the next assignment. Today, be a product specialist but layer on a geographic orientation.

Rod's Reflections:

Market expertise is important, but it's not the only thing you should look for in a broker that could deliver value for you. Look at their track record and the kinds of transactions that they have closed. Pay attention to how the broker describes things when you ask them how the market is. Do they speak in vague generalities using adjectives or do they answer with specifics, using statistics? Evaluate their negotiating skills, communication skills, and creativity. Ask yourself whether the broker you're considering has demonstrated honesty and integrity. Did they give you sound advice, even when it was not in their best interest to do so? If the answer is "no," run the other way.

Rod's Wrap-Up

Scoring a pot of gold is great, but real life rarely turns out the way it does in fairy tales. If you're a broker, find the situation where you do your best and can deliver the most value to your clients. What real value is the brokerage platform bringing to your personal practice? How do you help them and how do they help you?

If you're an investor, seek out a broker who can deliver the most value to you. How will you know if they can and will? Have they done it for others in your market? How have they kept in touch with you, regularly or sporadically? Ask to speak to other clients the broker has worked with. Any broker who is a true expert will have dozens of past clients who would love to speak to you.

In September of 2018, Bob took 53 people who had been with him at Cushman & Wakefield and Massey Knakal and moved to JLL. What he thought was originally the best decision for everyone turned out to be the wrong decision for him based on what would happen less than a year after that move. There would be more challenges fitting in at another large firm. And the market was already in a historic correction that would include COVID and its aftermath.

THE BIGGEST CHANGES LEAD TO THE GREATEST GROWTH OPPORTUNITIES

The next few years of Bob's career would be filled with both triumph and tribulation. Change is hard, even for the best brokers in the world. Bob's moved to JLL with great hope. The existing JLL investment sales business was small and only marginally productive. The 53 colleagues Bob brought with him to JLL would certainly change the nature of the second-largest commercial brokerage company on the globe. At first, great things were happening, and the work ecosystem was progressing nicely.

Then in June 2019, the NYS legislature dramatically changed the rent regulation system in New York, completely upending the largest product submarket in the city by far. Apartment building sales had always been a big part of Bob's practice, but what would the future hold here?

Then in July 2019, JLL announced it was acquiring HFF, but on the condition that HFF management would run everything. HFF had its roots in the mortgage brokerage business, but its investment sales platform was not even considered a runner-up in the New York City market.

Under HFF's leadership, JLL's capital markets business had a new structure and culture. In addition, the investment sales market landscape was changing. And then came the pandemic, something unlike anything in modern history, that brought real estate transactions, and most of life's assumed givens, to a complete halt.

Bob needed to navigate uncharted territory and find new opportunities. What he did would profoundly change his brokerage practice. He would do something he had wanted to do for decades, even though it would take a massive effort and not pay off for years. What he did ultimately reinforced his position as New York's premier commercial real estate broker.

Different Specialties Within Commercial Brokerage

One of the biggest lessons of this book, and something that became crystal clear to me by trying to make the JLL experience work, is understanding the profound differences between different specialties within commercial brokerage. Office leasing, mortgage brokerage, and investment sales are completely different businesses, and a single approach and philosophy for managing them is misguided and ineffective.

Office leasing is a business that requires national, if not a global presence if you want to work with the largest tenants. They have offices in many cities and countries and often want to work with the same company in every market. There are also a host of services a large brokerage can provide for the tenant that are symbiotic with leasing. These include project management, development services for tenant installations, consulting and a host of others. Having a big firm that has integrated service lines and geographic locations is extraordinarily helpful.

The mortgage brokerage business has similar attributes. It shocked me that when I spoke to the mortgage brokers at JLL who were based in New York City, that about 75% of their business was being done outside of New York. Apparently, this was the case for their mortgage brokers around the country. Understanding this made me realize why the company (HFF) operated the way it did and why HFF had never really been a factor in the New York City investment sales market. It operated like a national debt business, not an investment sales business.

The investment sales business is hyperlocal. With the exception of brokers who focus on triple net-leased assets, an investment sales broker can't consistently do deals outside of their area without some boots on the ground or local market knowledge. I know very few sales brokers who operate in multiple markets—if they are not running around representing buyers. But if you are trying to maximize the price for your seller, you must know the local market intimately.

And really, if you think about it, it's not the brokerage firm that provides the expertise but the individual broker. Moreso than any other discipline in brokerage, sales brokerage is much more of an individual business where the individual broker makes all the difference. Most clients don't care what firm someone is at, and the big firms can't get their minds around that.

Further, there is a big difference between experience and expertise. When a potential seller is thinking about whether or not to sell their building, they must rely on an individual investment broker who has both experience and expertise in their product type. The broker's firm doesn't sell the asset; the individual broker does. Specialization, experience, and expertise all make a huge difference.

For me, it's simple. I sell buildings in New York City. If you want to buy or sell your building in Dubuque, you need a broker who's an expert in that market and in that product type. The subtlety is that product specialization is the most important aspect of specialization today, but it is imperative to have a geographical overlay also – in most product types. The point is, as a broker, you still have to operate within a certain geography, but just ideally doing one product type within that geography.

Why Specialization Multiplies Effort

This perspective comes from the realization that brokers have two main assets, their knowledge and their time. We are always trying to increase our knowledge base, but how do we create more time? The only way is to use your time more effectively. The product specialization approach achieves this.

For example, if last week a broker closes on three sales, an apartment building, a retail property, and an office building and is pitching an office building this week – the seller doesn't want to hear about the apartment building sale or the retail property sale. They want to hear everything about the office building sale. Two-thirds of the broker's activity last week is not helping get this week's assignment. If however, the broker sold three office buildings last week, 100% of their time was accretive towards getting this week's assignment. This is how a broker "creates" time.

By specializing on product type, one hundred percent of what you do all day is accretive to your knowledge base, your track record, and getting that next deal.

~

Rod's Reflections:

Bob's entrepreneurial nature would have made fitting into a corporate culture of any kind difficult. JLL has a particular way of doing things they reasonably expect brokers to adapt to, and it works for them. But the way Bob has operated for decades has worked for him and made him one of the top investment sales brokers in the world. A clash of perspectives was inevitable.

Things got even more difficult because Bob's time at JLL overlapped with a unique time in New York City and commercial real estate. The pandemic was an externality that no one anticipated, and no one knew how to react to it.

The Pandemic

So, we got to JLL in September of 2018. By 2019, the cracks in the sales market started to break through, particularly in multifamily, which is the biggest submarket in New York by number of properties by a wide margin. It was more severe than it might have been because of draconical changes in the rent regulation laws. The sales market for apartment buildings, by far the largest subset of buildings, essentially shut down as market participants tried to figure out the impacts of the new changes to the rules of the game. Then, in March 2020, the Pandemic hit, and we were all told to leave the office for two weeks to let the virus "pass over us" and "flatten the curve". We were told to go home and hunker down.

I was not feeling well and called my doctor. The symptoms were slight. I felt fine other than losing my sense of smell. He told me to just monitor things and keep in touch with him a couple of times per day. He also mentioned that he had heard New York City might quarantine Manhattan and that I should take my family up to our country house in Connecticut asap. Within an hour, we were on the road.

But before we get into that, let's think about the impact on the commercial real estate market. If there's no foot traffic, and stores are closed, how can retailers make money? How are they going to pay the rent? What impact would this have on property owners? And it quickly became clear that this was going to be more than just a two-week shutdown.

Nobody was going back to the office. You had this weird dynamic in office buildings where you had economic occupancy but not physical occupancy. Sure, tenants were paying rent (or at least they were supposed to be. Many were not.), but no one was actually in the office. So, the question every investor had was, okay, we have economic occupancy, we don't have physical occupancy, but what happens when the lease expires? What will the absorption of vacant space be like? Some tenants stopped paying rent.

Residential properties were not immune. When residential tenants' leases expired, they overwhelmingly didn't renew them. They went to live with mom and dad. Or they went to the boroughs for more space with a home office. Many went to apartments and houses in New Jersey, Long Island, and Westchester. Many moved out, and many of those that stayed, stopped paying rent.

How can you determine a building's value if tenants are not paying, or might stop paying, rent? Sales volumes dropped like a stone.

The only real estate markets that did well in 2020 and 2021 were the suburban residential rental and single-family home markets because people moved out of the city and rented an apartment or bought a house. There was a mass exodus from rental apartments, and vacancy in Manhattan soared. Residential rents dropped by 30%.

From October 2015 through the first quarter of 2021, we were in a correction catalyzed by oversupply, overinvestment, and natural market cyclicality, which was exacerbated by the pandemic. That period, from October 2015 through March 2021, was the longest correction we'd ever seen. From October of 2015 through February of 2020, it was mostly a volume correction and then when the Pandemic came along, it converted the mostly volume correction into a value correction. It seemed like it would never end. Even the Savings & Loan Crisis in the early nineties was only four years long. This was much longer.

Rod's Reflections:

Market cycles have always been part of commercial real estate. The correction from 2015 through 2021 was longer than most, but it was still a basic market correction. The pandemic was a once-in-a-

generation trial that affected commercial real estate and every other aspect of society.

Businesses of all kinds sent people home in March 2020. Because the government told us so, we expected this would be over soon. We expected to be back at work in a few weeks. On April 12th, 2020, Anthony Fauci told CNN that a return to normalcy was imminent. He said, "It could possibly start at least in some ways, maybe next month." He was wrong.

Let me use Bob's sales figures to illustrate how hard the pandemic hit many people in commercial real estate. In 2019, Bob sold 39 buildings. But in 2020 he sold only 8, his lowest figure in 30 years, except for the 7 he sold in 1990 during the S&L Crisis. Put this in context. Over his 40-year career, Bob was selling more than 1 building per week, on average. In 2020, he sold less than 1 building every six weeks. Again, New York City became a ghost town; no one knew how to value properties, and the market sucked.

There was also personal turmoil for Bob. JLL moved quickly to lay off people, including some who had come over with Bob from Cushman & Wakefield. These were folks that Bob had worked with for many years, even back to the Massey Knakal days. They were good, experienced people. It didn't matter, they were gone. The place that they thought would be safe in tough times turned out not to be so safe after all. As Bob shared with me, "At public companies, it's all about the stock price. We thought at a big shop, we would be okay if a downturn hit. As it turns out, they cut faster than anyone else."

The crisis was a mix of danger and opportunity. Bob has always been able to spot the opportunity amidst the danger. The pandemic offered him an opportunity to do something he'd always wanted to do, and it would lead to one of the great, if not the greatest, innovations of his career.

The Opportunity of a Lifetime

We thought we'd be back in the office in two weeks, but that didn't happen, and when it became clear it would be a while, I needed to go back to our city apartment to get some stuff we would need as we left Manhattan in such a rush.

My drive back to the city was surreal. There were hardly any cars on I-95. What normally takes 2 ½ hours took just an hour and a half. As I pulled off the FDR Drive onto East 71st Street, I felt like I was on a movie set. New York City turned into a ghost town. No cars on the streets moving, no stores opened, no people walking around, Nothing.

Before I got to my apartment, it occurred to me that this was a once-in-a-lifetime opportunity to do something I had wanted to do for over ten years. I needed to take advantage of this amazing opportunity. If I was ever going to do a physical count of every building under construction, this was the perfect opportunity.

The Land Market in New York City

A big part of my practice, and a growing part of my practice for years, had been land sales. In order to really do a BOV (Broker

Opinion of Value) and evaluate land properly, you need to know what the supply pipeline looks like so you know what the competitive set will look like for any particular building once it gets built. But the data was shockingly difficult to find.

And a big part of the problem with understanding the land market in NY is that different product sectors operate differently. New York City has a big advantage over many municipalities in that it is an as-of-right zoning jurisdiction. There is no "entitlement" process to go through. Zoning here tells you what type of building you can build (commercial, residential, industrial, etc.), how large a building you can build (for every square foot of land, there is a multiple to calculate buildable footage), and what shape the building can have. All you have to do is get your building plans approved by the city to make sure the building conforms to the building code. The rest is already in place.

Most firms will tell you that land in Manhattan averaged $X per buildable square foot last year. The problem with that is you are mixing several different product types. This is similar to me telling you that last year, the average price of a peach, a bowling ball, and a 2" x 4" was $11.50. That number is meaningless.

I have always felt that going out to do a physical count was the only way to do this. But who has the time to do that? The pandemic was the perfect opportunity. Sales activity dropped to a trickle, the streets were empty, and getting around Manhattan would never be easier. I had to take advantage of this.

Walking the Streets

I decided I would walk the most prime streets of Manhattan from 96th Street south on the east side and 110th Street south on the west side. I immediately called my sales team manager and asked him to have the guys make copies of the Manhattan version of the Sanborn Land Book, which is a very detailed map of every block, showing the outline of each tax parcel as well as information about the size, layout, and height of each building on the parcels. The book is big, with each page measuring about 28" x 18", and each page contains about 12 to 20 blocks, depending on the size of those blocks.

My idea was to go into the field with copies of those pages and highlight the buildings I saw that were actively under construction to create a pipeline of supply coming to the market. Within five minutes, I realized the opportunity was much larger than just creating a pipeline of construction. I also thought highlighting the maps would be easier than writing notes on a pad. And this way, I made sure that no blocks were overlooked.

Each day we were in the field, we would bring a batch of pages from the Sanborn Book, many highlighters, bottles of water, and lunch as no stores were open and there was no place to buy a sandwich. I ended up taking pictures of all these sites and cataloging everything. It was easy because nobody was on the street. Over a four-month period, we spent 220 hours in the field and looked at all 27,649 buildings south of 96th Street and 110th Street. The only problem I had was that no retail stores were open, no hotels were open, so I had to go back to my apartment every time I had to use a bathroom. I got out to the streets in mid-April and finished up in

August. It was, by far and away, the best work I have ever done. At the time I had lived in Manhattan for 37 years and walked down streets I never even knew existed. I wish I had done this decades earlier.

As a broker, prospecting for properties for sale has always been the most important revenue-generating activity for me. From the time I started making cold calls in 1984, I had created catalogs with a page for each property. Each page had a photo, tax lot map, and ownership information, along with a place to write notes regarding the results of those calls. The goal was 8 connections per day back then. Over time the goal rose from 40 to 50 connections per week. Ever since the Pandemic, when I had very few interruptions (working from home, I was actually much more productive), I have been achieving over 100 connections per week with property owners.

More Opportunities

Being out in the field and looking at every property looking for buildings under construction afforded me another great opportunity. I could identify *potential* development sites. Those would be sites where the existing building was built to only a fraction of its maximum density per our as-of-right zoning. Understanding zoning in various parts of the city made this possible with visual inspection. A building that is one or two stories in a district that allows for high density is a no-brainer to identify.

And there was another opportunity: to identify potential "assemblage sites". Clearly, Manhattan doesn't have rolling acreage of undeveloped land (other than Central Park), so to create a development site, often a number of smaller properties have to be purchased or "assembled" to be demolished to create a piece of land on which to build a new building.

So, the exercise grew in scope, and I highlighted every building under construction or demolished in green, every single property development site where the improvements were small relative to its potential density in orange, and potential assemblage sites in yellow.

I was not only coming up with information to construct an accurate development pipeline but also coming up with a specific set of potential sites to make prospecting calls to. This was turning into a much more valuable initiative than I ever imagined.

Categorizing the Data

When we finally got to the southern tip of Manhattan, it was time to figure out exactly what we had.

When we put our dataset together, we disaggregated the information into five main buckets: 1) residential rental, 2) residential condo, 3) hotel, 4) office and 5) miscellaneous to include everything that doesn't fit into the first four buckets like education and hospitality. So, when we look at land, we look at it through that prism.

And then we needed data for each of those buckets with regard to the construction pipeline. The difficulty is that with the exception of residential condos, there is little information published about the construction status within the other buckets that is publicly available and that can be relied on. And even on the condo side, while every major residential brokerage firm publishes a condo pipeline report, they vary widely. One report will say that there are 6,000 units in the pipeline, and another will say 9,000. A third firm might have something very different.

Why? Because methodology determines results. What size buildings do you count? When do you start counting a building? Is it when the developer buys the site? When the developer starts selling? When the building gets the temporary certificate of occupancy? If you have a building being developed with 100 condo apartments but the developer only puts 15 on the market initially, how many do you count? And when do you stop counting a unit – when it goes under contract? When it closes? Methodology determines everything. Using different methodologies is why the residential brokerage reports are so different.

We began to do research on each of the highlighted properties.

For the sites highlighted in green, we researched each one to determine the builder, when they bought the site, what they were planning to build on it, etc. We obtained similar information for the sites that had been demolished but were not yet under construction. We created a bucket of "pending sites" where a developer purchased, or owned, the site and that pending site flipped into the "active" bucket when a construction loan was obtained.

For the properties in orange, we researched ownership information and created a catalog with information about every owner. We also created what we called a "one-pager", which had a copy of the tax lot map, a photograph, and the ownership information. These were put into three-ring binders, which I use for prospecting purposes.

The yellow sites were much more difficult to research. On a typical blockfront along an avenue, there may be as many as ten properties. If there were 10 separate owners of those properties, this was a very low-probability assemblage opportunity, so those blocks were discarded. However, if one owner owned multiple properties, that became an opportunity for us to prospect to try to create a development site through the assemblage process.

We followed up the 220 hours in the field with about 3000 hours of research over the next two years or so. Since the field work was completed, we stayed on top of all demolition permits and construction permits to stay current with the most recent developments. Today, we have the construction pipeline within each bucket down to the square inch.

The Knakal Map is Born and Develops

To get a better perspective on certain neighborhoods, I ended up taping three or four sections of the map together to examine what was happening in a particular neighborhood. That was such an interesting and insightful exercise that I continued to add sections of the map together, and before I knew it, the entire thing was taped together and measured 24 feet long and 10 feet wide.

So, I had this giant map, and my idea was to take it to client's offices when I was going to make a presentation. But how was I going to get this massive map around town? I rolled it up on an 8' wooden closet rod, which was about as big as I could get into the car. That necessitated folding it once to bring the Lower East Side (which protrudes further to the east than the rest of Manhattan) over the rest of the map. The unfortunate thing was that most clients didn't have a conference table big enough to accommodate the thing. When I was on my way to a meeting with a property owner, I got caught in the rain. The map was getting wet, and I realized the map needed a home somewhere.

JLL didn't want to give me a big enough space, so I went out and rented a space large enough to layout the map, got a bunch of tables, laid the map out, put Plexiglas on top of it, and started inviting clients to come over. I handled the appropriate licensing requirements so I could do business out of the space and alerted JLL that I was going to be working out of the space part of the time and set up shop. I started calling it "The Knakal Map Room," originally in "an undisclosed location" because we didn't have our backup systems in place, and I didn't want anyone to steal the map. The mystery about the "undisclosed location" added to the allure for market participants.

We started having clients come over, and they were blown away. There is nowhere else in the city to get this type of perspective on the market. That perspective is backed up with incredible data and research, some of which goes back to 1984 and that I had kept in boxes and have now digitized.

The Map has turned out to be a very helpful tool for day-to-day prospecting. I'm calling, and I am physically kneeling on top of the table, probably once or twice a day, looking at something. On almost every phone call I have with a potential seller, I'm looking at their property on The Map and everything going on around it.

We most recently enhanced the map by using different-colored Post-Its™ to identify comparable sales and sites for sale. It's tremendously insightful and, more importantly, demonstrates that we know everything there is to know about Manhattan's land market. Ultimately, this knowledge helps our clients make more informed, and therefore, better decisions.

Rod's Reflections:

The Knakal Map Room is an amazing achievement. In some ways, Bob's entire life and career prepared him for it. He started working for CB as a summer intern cataloging buildings in Morris County, New Jersey, using the old Hagstrom maps to get around. In the early days of Massey Knakal, he created what he called "catalogs" with a building's picture and lots of relevant data. His career and land assemblage deals taught him what was important. The pandemic provided the opportunity and the time to bring it all together.

Winston Churchill is often credited with the saying that we shape our tools, and then our tools shape us. That was certainly the case with Bob and the Knakal Map Room. He developed it for one purpose and along the way he found many more ways it would enhance his business and help his clients make the best decisions possible.

Developing The Knakal Map Room was only one driver of the triumph and tribulation that was 2023. The other was social media. As innovative as Bob is, he was a social media novice. That would change dramatically in 2023.

Social Media

I'm terrible with technology. On my annual summary of strengths and weaknesses, using technology has been on top of the weaknesses column for many years. I held onto my flip phone way longer than I should have just because I was used to it. I held onto my Blackberry for much longer than I should have because I liked the buttons. I just upgraded my iPhone because my phone wasn't modern enough to do things I wanted to do. Go on a device and chat with people via social media. Yeah, right!

But I saw what Rod was doing on social media and spoke to him at length about it and that was inspiring. Rod, to his credit, has embraced technology and told me I had to adapt if I wanted to survive.

I met Mo Regalado, who handles some social media for Rod at MassimoCon and got to know her a little bit. People had been after me for years to become more active. I'd be out for drinks with people and tell a story about a deal and people would love them and often suggested that I should share these stories on social media. It was time to give it a try. I thought, hey, let's try it for three months and see what happens. January 1, 2023, was my first real day. I had LinkedIn and Twitter accounts for years but had never gone on them and would just have our PR folks post the usual: "I just listed this" and "I just sold that".

Prior to getting active, I looked at the platforms with Mo and looked at what other brokers were doing. I wanted to try to be a bit different. But what could I bring to the table? I had experience. I had sold a lot of buildings, I owned and ran a business of 250 people, I spent a lot of time watching brokers perform, I tried to constantly motivate the troops, and I wrote hundreds of articles about commercial real estate. I thought that I could share some of this with the various social media communities.

I had no idea that it would turn out the way it did.

At the start of 2023, I had virtually no presence on any social media. Rod, Mo, and I mapped out a strategy and started implementing it in January 2023, when I had just under 5,500 followers on Twitter and maybe the same on LinkedIn. As of the writing of this book, I have close to 100,000 followers on all my social platforms. In fact, CREi just named me the #1 commercial real estate influencer on LinkedIn for 2024, the #2 commercial real estate influencer on X (formerly Twitter) for 2024 and #8 on Instagram. By the end of 2024, in aggregate on my social media platforms, I had 21.8 million impressions. These impressions are helping to strengthen my personal brand and are leading to business opportunities that I never would have gotten.

The positive feedback has been great, and the opportunities that I have been exposed to have been overwhelming. At JLL, in almost 6 years, I never received any feedback from management at all, good or bad. The positive feedback I was getting from social media was feeding the human need to be appreciated and heard. So, because it was satisfying that human desire, I wanted it more and more, and I think that is one of the reasons I have become so passionate about it.

Many of the things we posted on social media were about The Knakal Map Room, which generated lots of buzz and queries. I discovered that social media is great for building a personal brand. It's another place an investor can look to find out about me and what people in the industry think of me.

More importantly, I realized how much my personal following on social media helps me get access to more resources for my clients. And the most important thing in the brokerage world is creating the best possible results for your client. The more you are "out there," the more information you get in the way of, and the more information you have, the more informed you can make your client. The more informed the client is, the better decisions they can make. It is, as economists refer to it, a "positive feedback loop".

The End at JLL

In Early February of 2024, I received a call from my good friend at CNBC, Brian Sullivan. They were doing a piece on commercial real estate and wanted me to appear. Naturally, I jumped at the opportunity. The morning after I appeared, I received a call from JLL's PR department. The new head of PR told me that it was wrong for me to go on national television without "permission". I told her that market exposure was a key to my brokerage practice and had been for decades and my contract stated that I had "unfettered access to the press and media". I was told that could not possibly be the case and that she would get right back to me. I didn't hear a word. Market presence is critically important to brokers, particularly in investment sales as "it's not who you know, it's who knows you"! This approach has gotten me quoted, or mentioned, in the media over 2,000 times per year.

On February 11, 2024, the New York Times published an article about The Knakal Map Room and I titled "This Real Estate Kingpin Maps Out the Path to Megadeals." The Times' Matthew Haag opened the piece with, "The best view of New York City might just be in a near-windowless conference room on the 12th floor of a Midtown Manhattan office building." Matthew was a social media follower and became intrigued by all of the coverage The Knakal Map Room was getting.

It was hard to imagine any free publicity that could be better for my business or my clients. Especially in the New York Times which rarely does profiles on anyone, let alone a real estate broker. Three days later, JLL fired me without notice.

Looking back, it's easy to see that big corporate firms were not a good place for me. I have to say probably the time that I enjoyed the most was at MK when we were at 70 or 80 people (we eventually got to 250) because I knew everybody really, really well. I knew the spouses' names, the kids' names, where they went to school, and even the dog's names. I loved the entrepreneurial energy and working hard with people I knew and liked. I liked making decisions quickly. The truth is, I just love being a broker and selling buildings. All of the corporate BS is not productive and can suck all of the energy out of the room. No thanks!

I really believe that big brokerage companies are where entrepreneurship goes to die. If you want to switch from Coke to Diet Coke in the kitchen, you send a memo to Cleveland, it goes to Singapore, comes back to Phoenix, and then you end up with Ginger Ale. And building value in yourself through personal branding is the most financially liberating thing you can do. Building a personal brand creates value and independence and will make you more valuable to your firm than the firm is to you. This is freedom - otherwise, you are a prisoner at the whim of your senior management.

Rod's Reflections:

I know what you are thinking. "Why would a CRE firm fire a top-performing broker?" Part of the answer is in the Commercial Observer's story about Bob's firing. The Observer's reporter heard the following from a source inside JLL.

"JLL has been consciously moving away from the historical model of focusing on individual brokers' star power to instead taking an investment banking approach, putting the client first, the firm second, and the individual broker last. JLL's management saw Knakal's Times article — which mentioned the brokerage only once — as the antithesis of that."

But here is the fact. Bob is a great broker, certainly the most prolific broker I have ever worked with. JLL is a great brokerage firm. One of the best commercial real estate brokerage organizations in the world. But it simply was not a fit. Think of Michael Jordan in a Los Angeles Lakers uniform. Both are great, but it just wasn't meant to be.

Rod's Wrap-Up

Probably the greatest missed opportunities happen when you aren't looking. Instead, you are panicking or focused on the wrong things. Market leaders have clarity amidst the chaos, which helps them seize or improve their leadership positions. When New York City was a ghost town, market activity was plummeting, and most were leaving the city or sequestered themselves in their homes; Bob took to the streets.

He worked tirelessly to pursue a vision although he didn't really understand the magnitude of his vision at the time. Cataloging led to the map, and the map led to The Knakal Map Room. Along the way Bob discovered more and more opportunities to leverage his effort.

The Knakal Map Room started in April 2020 and is still being developed today. Bob constantly makes enhancements and improvements to serve his clients better. Its creation has grabbed the attention of property investors around the globe. You can follow Bob on LinkedIn or Twitter (now 'X') to see all the folks who come to visit, learn from him, and admire his work.

It also grabbed the attention of the New York Times. The once-in-a-lifetime profile may have been the last straw for JLL, but it also became the catalyst for Bob's next stage: the creation of BKREA.

MAPPING OUT THE FUTURE

The commercial real estate business has undoubtedly changed since Bob arrived at Coldwell Banker on the first day of his first summer internship in 1981. When Bob showed up for his first full day of work at CB in Manhattan on July 16, 1984, there was no computer on his desk, no cell phone, and no fax machine. Brokers carried rolls of quarters around to make calls from telephone booths on street corners. You could tell the extent of a broker's network by looking at the size of their Rolodex™. Bob had two big Rolodexs™ on his desk by 1985.

The world has changed dramatically, and we must change with it. But as much as things change, some things remain the same. The fundamentals of the business are constant and haven't changed much since 1984.

Think about how Bob implements the basics. He collects, analyzes, interprets, and deploys information to deepen his expertise, keep up with a changing market, and puts his clients in the best possible position to make the best, most informed decisions.

There is one constant, and that is change. The market is constantly changing. As early as 1984, Bob realized he was not in the real estate business but instead in the information and relationship business. The fictional character, Gordon Gekko, from the 1987 movie "Wall Street", said, "Information is the most valuable commodity I know of." Bob agrees and constantly strives to have the best information in the market. In the early days, that meant knowing the details about every property and deal in his geographic territory. Today,

Bob uses sophisticated AI and other technologies to dive into the sea of data and develop meaningful insights.

Bob also devotes time, money, and energy to building his market presence. While traditional market presence initiatives might seem self-serving or ego-driven. Bob will be the first to tell you it's all about the client. It always has been and always will be. His deep-seated desire to be the best is palpable. He has an insatiable appetite to do better than his best every day. It has been a treat to see him in action. The behind-the-scenes stuff. It's like watching Kobe Bryant shoot free throws, hundreds of times per day after everyone else has left the court and the gym is empty, except for him.

These old, familiar pillars of success will be the foundation for the next phase of selling buildings. Of course, new strategies and tactics will be thrown in as he always seeks to stay ahead of the curve. It is his insatiable desire to succeed that continues to drive him.

What's Ahead

The world's changing, and you must stay ahead of everybody else. It's evolution or annihilation. AI is not going to replace anyone, but someone using AI will replace someone who doesn't. I see the future as clear as day, and it's all about taking advantage of technology. The changes to the business over the next five years are going to be mind-blowing. Technologies that are just two months old and seem cutting-edge are dinosaurs 60 days later, replaced by something bigger, better, faster, broader, and easier to use. The rate of change is staggering, and we have to stay on top of everything.

Think about the way that Massey Knakal kicked ass, right? We had better information than anyone else, had a business model that worked, were able to motivate our teammates by implementing a servant leadership management style, and were creating content before anyone, including us, knew that expression. We used that content to establish proof of capability and did it over and over and over again. Today, the concept is called "proof stacking." And we lapped the field by more than 3x – for 14 years in a row! That felt great. Winning feels great. I am addicted to it. And that's my goal for BKREA.

I want to achieve that same level of dominance because it feels great. Maybe not in terms of the total number of deals as we did at Massey Knakal because I don't want to have 250 employees again. The management level needed for that is not what I am looking for. I want to achieve a dominant position in the niches where we play. And we are well on the way!

In addition to using new technologies in new ways, social media will definitely be part of my future. 85 to 90 percent of my client base is not on social media yet. But I have not spoken to anybody in the past year who doesn't know what The Knakal Map Room is, which is shocking, right? Social media made that happen. The world is becoming smaller and smaller, and social media will continue to play a bigger and more prominent role. It is a vital part of a market presence campaign today but will be an even more critical part of creating a market presence in the future.

I reduced my time on social media compared to early 2023, and it feels much better. It's much more like I'm in the swing of doing business. Social media definitely helps your reputation, but like all things, we have to take it in moderation. Some business comes out of it, but nothing's better than working on deals and talking to clients.

To dominate the market, I need reliable data to turn into information by putting it in context and using maps to represent it clearly and understandably. Then, we add our knowledge and help our clients decide what to do. Here's an example of what's possible.

New York City currently has about 100 million square feet of vacant office space. There are only about six cities in the US that even have 100 million square feet of office space. We also desperately need housing. Converting vacant, functionally obsolete office buildings into apartments makes a ton of sense, and our policymakers seem to get it. But that is a very complicated business. Many factors need to be taken into consideration in addition to economic feasibility. Zoning regulations, tax abatements, building code requirements, bonus programs for additional density, and a host of other considerations that need to be analyzed. These things all vary from block to block. Even the most seasoned professionals are trying to figure this stuff out.

What did we do at BKREA? We have assembled a Policy and Zoning SWAT team of professionals, including property information scientists, zoning experts and attorneys (some of whom helped New York City write the rules), architects, and cost estimators. We are analyzing every building that an owner is considering selling to see what is physically possible and what the economic realities are. We are doing what a buyer would need to do, and it normally would take many weeks. We are doing the work in a matter of days and including it as part of our pitch to get retained. No one else is doing this.

Further, we are proactively doing feasibility studies for all Class B & C office buildings in Manhattan to determine which of four buckets each building falls into: 1) definitively can be converted, 2) can be converted with minor modifications to the exterior of the building, 3) can be converted with major modifications to the exterior of the building, and 4) definitely cannot be converted. We have a different prospecting marketing campaign to reach out to the owners of buildings within each of these buckets.

This is going to be big business for a long time.

We have the best data around because we've done the hard work of gathering, verifying, and organizing it so we can use it. All kinds of regulations determine what you can do, and there will be many more. So, if we can understand the ins and outs of it and all these new rules and regulations, we have a tremendous opportunity to help owners maximize their prices, giving us a competitive advantage.

We'll have the best, most reliable data. We can present that data to a client so that they understand the context. There's going to be an office conversion map room. Because we've done the work to understand the realities, we have the knowledge to help a client decide the best path forward. What we're going to do is put ourselves in a position where anybody who owns one of these buildings would be absolutely insane not to at least talk to us.

We have already achieved that position within the land sales market in Manhattan by virtue of The Knakal Map Room. We have the development pipeline nailed down to the square inch for residential rentals, residential condos, hotels, office buildings, and a fifth miscellaneous bucket.

We are also working on The Knakal Land Index, which will look at comparable development site sales within those five buckets going back to 1984. Yes, 40 years of land sales data, all analyzed using the same exact methodology. This study currently encompasses 2,417 transactions. No one else in the market has that data and analyzed it the way we have. This is another huge competitive advantage, and we are going to press that advantage into the outer boroughs.

We will also do the same thing we did with The Knakal Map Room, which is all about Manhattan, for Northern Manhattan, Brooklyn, Queens, and the Bronx. The possibilities are endless.

With all of the new things we are doing, I feel like I am starting over again—only this time with a 40-year track record behind me. I am just getting warmed up! There is so much to do and so much to achieve! Every day is like waking up to play the most exciting board game on earth—selling commercial real estate in New York City. Many of the seasoned brokers in my age cohort are retiring. That won't happen for me. I love what I do too much. Why would I ever stop?

Rod's Wrap-Up

The old, familiar pillars of success will be the foundation for the next phase of selling buildings. Of course, new strategies and tactics will be thrown in, as Bob always seeks to stay ahead of the curve.

You might expect Bob to slow down after forty years, but it's just the opposite. He says he's "just getting started." The fact is that Bob Knakal doesn't "do" brokerage, he IS brokerage. It's part of his identity.

Of course, Bob is mapping out a future for his firm, BKREA. He's always been willing to see the opportunity in hard times. It's exciting and inspiring to watch.

THE STRATEGIC INVESTOR'S SUCCESS MAP
13 CRITICAL LESSONS FOR SELLING BUILDINGS
BY BOB KNAKAL

Market intelligence and timing are fundamental to success in real estate investing.

In "The Birth of the Virgin Hotel" story, where the property went through multiple market cycles from 2006-2012, understanding market timing proved crucial. The initial buyer's default and $9.2M deposit loss during the market downturn, followed by Cal's patient approach to "sit on the asset until the market improved," demonstrates how recognizing market signals and having patience through cycles can create opportunities. This principle was also evident in the original deal price of $368/SF in 2007 compared to $287/SF in 2011.

Complex deal management capabilities set successful investors apart.

In "I'm Dying and My Sister is Killing Me!", the solution required understanding tenants-in-common ownership structures and partial interest sales. The "Birth of the Virgin Hotel" involved multiple properties, various transaction types, and creative deal structures. These stories show how understanding multiple transaction types and being willing to work through complexity creates value that others might miss.

Due diligence excellence is non-negotiable in successful real estate investing.

The "There are Almost Always Obstacles" story at 300 Livingston Street demonstrates this perfectly. Multiple complex issues affected the property: a 60+ year lease for loading docks, basement and underground passageway rights, subway line and MTA easement, and various height restrictions. TF Cornerstone's success came from their thorough due diligence and previous experience handling similar obstacles.

Value creation through problem-solving is a crucial skill that distinguishes successful investors.

In "Hey Baby, How About a Buyout?", the investor's creative approach to dealing with a holdout owner by threatening to build low-income housing nearby demonstrated strategic problem-solving. Similarly, in "The Birth of the Virgin Hotel", the solution to subdivide lots along zoning boundary lines created value by maximizing both residential and commercial components, allowing Lam Group to acquire what they needed while preserving value for other uses.

Understanding tenant dynamics is essential in today's market.

The "Hey Baby, How About a Buyout?" story vividly illustrates this, showing how even a single tenant can impact a $69.6M deal. The varying buyout costs - $150,000 for a pizza shop versus $850,000 for a single residential tenant - demonstrate the complexity of tenant rights and the importance of budgeting for tenant removal costs. The story also shows how even non-regulated tenants can create significant delays through legal claims.

Professional network development is crucial.

In "I'm Dying and My Sister is Killing Me!", the broker's understanding of legal structures and ability to work with various stakeholders unlocked the deal's potential. The "There are Almost Always Obstacles" story showed how success required coordinating with attorneys, architects, engineers, and adjacent property owners to overcome multiple challenges.

Deal structure flexibility often determines an investor's ability to close complex transactions.

In "The Birth of the Virgin Hotel", the final solution involved multiple creative elements: subdivision of lots, preservation of specific zoning rights, and a structure that satisfied both hotel developers and residential investors. The "You Can't Make This Up!" story about the church property demonstrated how having financial flexibility ($1.45M all-cash with 10 percent deposit) can strengthen negotiating position.

Market knowledge depth should be continuously developed.

The success of TF Cornerstone in the "There are Almost Always Obstacles" story came from their deep understanding of similar challenges in previous projects. In "Trust Your Advisors: How a Second Opinion Added $28.8 Million", the broker's knowledge of the emerging condo conversion trend added significant value that the original managing agent missed entirely.

Risk management is crucial for long-term success.

In "The Birth of the Virgin Hotel", story demonstrates this through Cal's decision to refuse a closing extension despite proof of funds, ultimately proving wise when the buyer defaulted. Similarly, in "Hey Baby, How About a Buyout!", understanding and budgeting for tenant removal risks was essential to the project's success.

Financial analysis skills are a must.

In "Trust Your Advisors", the difference between the managing agent's $17.5M offer and the final $46.3M sale price demonstrates the importance of proper valuation. The Virgin Hotel story's various price points across different zoning districts ($400/SF for residential versus $300/SF for commercial) shows the necessity of detailed financial analysis.

Strategic planning sets successful investors apart from speculators.

In "The Birth of the Virgin Hotel", the long-term approach to assemblage over many years, including waiting through market cycles and negotiating multiple transactions, demonstrates the importance of strategic patience. The "There are Almost Always Obstacles" story shows how proper planning and sequencing of solutions led to success.

Relationship building is often overlooked but crucial.

The story of Benjamin Aryeh in "I'm Dying and My Sister is Killing Me!" shows how maintaining professional relationships and trust (paying commission early) leads to future opportunities. "The Birth of the Virgin Hotel", story's success relied heavily on relationships built over years with multiple property owners.

Technical expertise development should be ongoing.

Every deal story demonstrates this need, but particularly "There are Almost Always Obstacles", where success required an acute understanding of zoning, subway infrastructure, air rights, and construction limitations. The Virgin Hotel deal similarly required expertise in zoning, air rights, and development regulations to maximize value through creative subdivision.

These lessons emphasize that successful commercial real estate investing requires a comprehensive approach combining market knowledge, technical expertise, relationship building, and strategic thinking. Success comes from understanding both the broader market dynamics and the specific details of individual deals while maintaining flexibility in approach and a willingness to solve complex problems.

THE BROKER'S SUCCESS MAP
13 ESSENTIAL BROKERAGE LESSONS: BK'S DEAL STORIES
BY ROD SANTOMASSIMO

Market expertise and value creation *are fundamental to broker success. In "Trust Your Advisors: How a Second Opinion Added $28.8 Million," Bob's knowledge of the emerging condo conversion trend enabled him to increase value by nearly $29M over the managing agent's offer. Similarly, in "The Birth of the Virgin Hotel," understanding different zoning districts and their impact on value allowed for creative subdivision solutions that maximized returns for all parties.*

Persistence and long-term relationship-building prove invaluable*. The "I'm Dying, and My Sister is Killing Me!" story shows how years of consistent contact and market updates led to trust, with the client keeping all the broker's mailings in a file even when not responding. Though risky, the personal visit to Connecticut broke through years of resistance because of the foundation laid through consistent communication.*

Creative problem-solving distinguishes top brokers from average ones*. In "There are Almost Always Obstacles" at 300 Livingston Street, the broker's understanding of zoning, infrastructure constraints, and development potential led to matching the property with TF Cornerstone, who had specific expertise in handling similar challenges. The Virgin Hotel deal's creative subdivision along zoning boundaries solved seemingly intractable problems.*

***Marketing process excellence is crucial for maximizing value**. In "Trust Your Advisors," the comprehensive marketing process generated 53 offers and multiple bidding rounds, compared to the managing agent's limited exposure to just three buyers. The "Virgin Hotel" story shows how broad marketing to the right buyer pool - in this case, hotel developers for one portion and residential developers for another - maximizes potential.*

***Professional composure and negotiation skills often determine success**. The "You Can't Make This Up!" story about the church property sale demonstrates how maintaining professional composure during difficult negotiations (even with a seller screaming and running out of the closing room) leads to successful outcomes. The Virgin Hotel deal required delicate negotiations across multiple parties over several years.*

***You must constantly maintain and demonstrate deep market knowledge.** In "There are Almost Always Obstacles," the broker's ability to identify and reach out to buyers with specific expertise in handling complex site issues proved crucial. Understanding both technical aspects (zoning, air rights) and market dynamics (buyer capabilities, pricing trends) allowed for matching the right buyers with the right opportunities.*

***Client advisory focus separates great brokers from mere transaction agent**s. In "Hey Baby, How About a Buyout!" advising the client to pay whatever is necessary for tenant buyouts ($850,000 for one tenant) because of the high sale price ($926 per buildable square foot) showed putting client interests first. Similarly, advising Cal to reject the buyer's extension request in the Virgin Hotel deal protected the client's interests.*

Creating competitive environments maximizes results. *The church property story shows how maintaining multiple interested parties prevented last-minute price reductions. The "Trust Your Advisors" story demonstrated how broad marketing and multiple bidding rounds drove the price from $17.5M to $46.3M through competitive tension.*

Communication and documentation skills prove essential. *Throughout the Virgin Hotel assemblage, clear communication of complex zoning issues, development potential, and deal structures kept all parties aligned. The ability to explain complicated situations simply and maintain clear documentation through multi-year deals ensures success.*

Understanding strategic timing and market cycles significantly affect outcomes. *In the Virgin Hotel story, understanding when to pause marketing during market downturns and when to re-engage as conditions improved maximized value. Similar timing expertise in "Trust Your Advisors" caught the condo conversion trend early.*

Professional network development creates deal flow and solutions. *The "$28.8 Million Question" came through attorney Andy Albstein's referral, demonstrating how professional networks generate opportunities. The "Almost Always Obstacles" story showed how relationships with attorneys, architects, and engineers helped solve complex problems. This is even more apparent with BK's recent surge in his social media presence.*

Client relationship management requires constant attention. *In "I'm Dying, and My Sister is Killing Me!" years of consistent contact and market updates-built trust that eventually led to the transaction.*

The Virgin Hotel story shows how maintaining relationships with multiple owners eventually enabled the complex assemblage.

Market presence and credibility building pay long-term dividends*. Throughout these stories, consistent market updates, professional marketing materials, and regular communication established credibility, leading to transactions years later. Even seemingly unresponsive clients, like in the Connecticut story, often paid attention to market presence efforts.*

These lessons demonstrate that successful commercial real estate brokerage requires a comprehensive approach combining market expertise, relationship building, technical knowledge, and unwavering focus on client interests. The most successful brokers maintain high professional standards, constantly expand their knowledge base, and focus on creating value through careful attention to both details and relationships. As seen in these stories, success often comes from years of groundwork, culminating in significant transactions that benefit all parties involved.

BROKER BONUS
THE BROKER'S DOZEN
HOW TO MAKE MORE MONEY IN LESS TIME
BY ROD SANTOMASSIMO

This section was written for brokers reading this book. If you're not a broker, read on anyway. These principles apply to any service business.

Hard work is necessary, but it's not enough. In the ever-evolving commercial real estate (CRE) world, success hinges on hard work and smart strategies. Here are twelve key ideas to help you make more money in less time, transforming your brokerage practice into a thriving, commission-driving machine.

Command Your Calendar. *Effective time management is the foundation of productivity. Allocate time for high-value activities like finding, winning, and fulfilling business. Don't let distractions dictate your schedule. Be intentional about your time. Focus on tasks that directly contribute to your success.*

At Massimo, we instill an I.P.A.I.D. approach to time utilization (Identify, Prioritize, Allocate, Implement, Delegate). The commission world is a long-pay game. Follow this approach, and you can say yes to the question, "Was I paid today?"

Engage Your Inactive Clients. *At Massimo, we don't believe in "past" clients. Considering your clients as past is like telling yourself they are dead to you. So, "past" becomes "passed." Instead, always* *remember that they are still your clients. They are simply not currently active. Refer to these "past clients" as "inactive clients."*

Your inactive clients are a goldmine of potential business. Implement strategies to retain and expand relationships with them. Remember, they are not just past deals but prospects for future opportunities. Keeping in touch and providing ongoing value can convert them into loyal repeat clients.

Get Off the Transaction Treadmill. *Getting caught up in the daily grind of closing deals is easy. However, it is crucial to take time to work* ***on*** *your business rather than just* ***in*** *it. This means strategizing, planning, and developing systems that allow your business to grow sustainably and efficiently. It is impossible to scale your business without processes.*

And even if you manage to do so, you still live in the whirlwind. Remember, treadmills don't go anywhere. Here's a hint. If you find yourself telling everyone you're busy, but your income is stuck, and your pipeline sucks – you are on the transaction treadmill.

Define Your Ideal Client. *Clarity is power. Clearly define your ideal clients and tailor your marketing efforts to attract them. Understand their needs, pain points, and what drives them. By focusing on your target audience, you can position yourself as an expert in your niche, making attracting the clients you want to work with easier.*

You need to go deep here. Work to understand their fears and frustrations as well as their goals and aspirations. The better you know your target market, the easier you will find crafting messages and a value proposition that will resonate with them.

Think Campaign. *Finding business isn't just about making cold calls; it's about creating a comprehensive plan to secure meetings. Think of your efforts as campaigns, with coordinated actions and messaging designed to reach and resonate with your target audience. This approach increases the likelihood of meaningful engagements. Today, many platforms will help you automate and coordinate your prospecting efforts.*

Yes, you will still have control of the conversations and correspondence, but you can reach thousands of prospects in minutes. At Massimo, we have developed AI-enhanced campaigns that include email, text correspondence, voice messaging, and live calls. While this is certainly not for all audiences, with or without AI integration, automated campaigns are a great accelerator.

You are Your Best Client. *This one is hard to swallow for many at first, but here is a fact about any sales or service position: You are your best client. No one will ever make more money for you than you. I see way too many brokers who have gotten into the business for personal freedom and released themselves from the tyranny of an employer, only to become employees of their clients.*

No single client will make you more money than all your clients over your career. You must, and I mean must, ***put yourself first****. Yes, you should be responsive and professional, of course. But you are building a business; you are the CEO of yourself.* ***You can't command your calendar if you don't define your priorities.***

Don't Be Invisible. *As Bob stated throughout this book, and I told him early in our relationship, it's not just about who you know; it's about who knows you. Build your brand and visibility in the market.*

Find another firm if your brokerage firm restricts you from building your brand. Seriously. See "You are Your Best Client."

Your brand is your value. Yes, there are several incredible institutional brokerage firms, and if you are aligned with any of them, leverage their strong brands, but don't forget your brand will be with you forever. This includes networking, speaking at industry events, and leveraging social media. Being visible makes it easier for potential clients to find and trust you.

Prune Your Pipeline. *Your pipeline is your business's lifeline. Regularly update and manage it to ensure you're not wasting time on deals that won't close. Focus on moving transactions forward and nurturing relationships.* ***A healthy pipeline is essential for consistent business growth.*** *Here's a test. Look at your pipeline right now. Which opportunities are you sorry you took? Which clients have been a pain in your butt? Remember, you are your best client.*

You are the CEO; as CEO, you get to fire any clients you wish, and at any time you want to. Way too many brokers ***allow their loyalty to diminish their royalties.*** *Who is more important than that troubling client or your spouse and kids? If you can't do this, read the next item more than once.*

Say No/Delegate. *When I first met Bob, he was everywhere and said yes to everyone. And he was tired. So, one of the first things I asked him to track was how often he said no. In fact, I challenged him to say no at least three times a week. And for Bob, who naturally loves people, it was HARD.*

Remember, in less than two years of our coaching, Bob doubled his income and tripled it within four. ***Recognize that you can't do everything yourself.*** *Delegate tasks that others can do better, faster, and more economically. This allows you to focus on high-value activities within your unique skill set. By the way, building a capable team is a wise investment in your business's success. Refer to "Command Your Calendar" and the "D" in I.P.A.I.D.*

Keep Score. *Tracking your activities and results is vital for understanding your progress. Without metrics, it's impossible to know what's working and what's not. Use data to make informed decisions, adjust your strategies, and continually improve your performance.*

Bob is a numbers guy. He loves stats and what they can tell him. I couldn't agree more, but sometimes, you can take a good thing too far. When I first met Bob, he was tracking over 100 weekly stats. Hell, he was tracking how many green juices he drank a week. Seriously, he did.

I got the 100+ weekly metrics down to 5 within a month. Now we have less. But here's the thing. When I compare our coaching clients, like Bob, who consistently track their weekly metrics to those who don't, ***those who track, make exponentially more than those who don't.*** *It's not even close. As they say, "You can't wing it to win it," so start tracking your numbers. Run your brokerage business like a business, not a hobby. Again, you are the CEO.*

Invest in You. *Your most valuable asset is yourself. Invest in your growth by seeking education, training, and mentorship. The more you learn and grow,* ***the more value you can provide to your***

clients and the more successful you will become. *Even Warren Buffett states that the best investment you can make is in yourself. Remember this: There are three intellects.*

Intellectual ignorance: you don't know what you don't know. None of us do.

Intellectual arrogance: you don't care about the first intellect and feel you're good enough without changing.

Intellectual curiosity: you recognize the first intellect, reject the second, ***and want to explore what is possible.***

There is only one path to exponential growth. Given that we are all ignorant, we have only two options: arrogant or curious. Which one are you? I would love for you to work with Massimo and our coaching staff.

Integrate artificial intelligence into your everyday practice. *As I shared in the final chapter of this book, Artificial Intelligence is here to stay. And very likely, from the time I typed this sentence to the time you are reading it, the capacity of AI will have increased a multitude of times. You have no choice. But I am not suggesting you figure it out. Get some help. My first AI mentor is more than 30 years younger than me. There are countless numbers of folks who can get you up to speed in no time. Just start and stay competitive as much as you can.*

Welcome to BFK. *When I was growing up in New York, we would order a dozen bagels and get thirteen; it was called a "baker's dozen." I am not sure if bakeries still do this. I've already given you a dozen* *proven ideas to increase the quality of your business and your life. This last idea is number thirteen, which makes this a baker's dozen, or, as I prefer, a "Broker's Dozen."*

Never forget that regardless of how bad a day you have or how big a deal may die, **it does not define you.** *I have seen Bob on the verge of tears, rage, and frustration many times since we started working together in 2011. Yes, even the most prolific brokers in the world have bad days, weeks, and months. Bob's career has put him in several positions to succeed, as it has put him in positions to fail.*

Sometimes I need to remind him that he is Bob Fucking Knakal and to stop feeling sorry for himself and move forward. More often, in celebration, I refer to him as "BFK."

If you have reached this point in the book, you are curious. You are not arrogant. You have the capability to be awesome! Never forget that. There will always be mistakes, but there is always time to grow.

Let's move forward - together.

Rod Santomassimo
Founder – The Massimo Group
and forever BFK's coach.

ABOUT THE AUTHORS

BOB KNAKAL

Bob Knakal has been a commercial real estate broker in NYC since 1984. During that time, he has brokered the sale of more than 2,342 buildings with a market value of approximately $22 billion.

For 26 years (1988-2014), he owned and ran Massey Knakal Realty Services, which sold more than three times the number of properties as the #2 firm in NYC from 2001 to 2014. He ran the firm with a Servant Leadership management style, empowering everyone on the team, intensely training them, and building their self-esteem, leading to this overwhelmingly dominant platform. The firm was sold to Cushman & Wakefield in 2014 for $100 million.

The Massey Knakal Legacy is illustrated by the fact that today, in the New York City investment sales market, 31 companies, or divisions of companies, are either owned by or run by folks who learned the business at Massey Knakal.

Bob is a prominent thought leader in the commercial real estate business, frequently writing about the market, lecturing on the market, and appearing on podcasts and national television shows on networks like Fox, CNBC, and MSNBC.

Recently, Bob started BKREA, an investment sales and capital markets brokerage firm in New York City. The firm combines best-in-class analog data sets with artificial intelligence technologies to create a new brokerage firm for a new era.

Bob is a graduate of the Wharton School at the University of Pennsylvania and is one of the most recognized and the most honored and awarded commercial real estate brokers in the world.

Bob lives in Manhasset, NY, with his wife, Cynthia, and his daughter Sophie.

For more information on Bob, including an extensive search on building sales in New York City, visit www.bobknakal.com

For assistance in selling your building at maximum value, visit www.BKREA.com

ROD SANTOMASSIMO

Rod Santomassimo is the founder of the Massimo Group, the premier coaching organization in the commercial real estate brokerage industry. The Massimo Group has assisted over 4,200 commercial real estate and mortgage brokers in building the business and life they desire.

Rod co-founded CREinvestorcoach.com, which assists brokers and non-brokers in entering or expanding their commercial real estate investment pursuits.

The author of four best-selling books – *Brokers Who Dominate, Teams Built to Dominate,* and *Knowing Isn't Doing* –became America's #1 sales book when it launched and *Dominators of Commercial Real Estate Brokerage.*

A graduate of Washington and Lee University, Rod earned his MBA from the Fuqua School of Business at Duke University, where he is a two-time recipient of the Duke University Fuqua School of Business Impact Alumni of the Year Award. Globe St. has recognized his contributions, designating him as a "Best Boss" in CRE.

Rod is a syndicated columnist for the New York Real Estate Journal and has been published and/or featured in several general business periodicals, including, but not limited to, Entrepreneur.com, The Good Men Project, and Thrive Global. He is also a CCIM and a patented inventor.

Rod is a sought-after speaker in the commercial real estate brokerage community and is known as a leader in artificial intelligence integration in CRE brokerage.

Rod lives in Cary, NC, with his wife, Launa. They have two adult children, Giana and Nicolas.

For more information on how you can build the commercial real estate brokerage business and life you have always desired, visit www.massimo-group.com.

www.ingramcontent.com/pod-product-compliance
Lightning Source LLC
LaVergne TN
LVHW020712110826
845149LV00012B/2222

* 9 7 9 8 9 9 2 9 0 0 1 0 1 *